From

MW01173322

"If you are anything like my wife and I, going through a devotional together has been tricky. Carla & Johnny created the solution in *From You & Me to We*. Their devotional finds the right balance of God's heart for marriage in relevant terms rooted in scripture while inviting couples to process with guided discussion questions. In an age where marriage and family are crumbling all around, this book will forge strong marriages to build strong families for generations to come."

— Jesse Jacobs, Campus Pastor at Grace Church San Diego

"Johnny and Carla Morton are living examples of how a strong, vibrant, Christ-centered marriage can be forged with intentionality. *From You & Me to We* is not just a marriage devotional; it is an expression of who they are as followers of Christ building their marriage on their relationship with the Lord and the Word of God. You won't find a more practical resource that will help you intentionally forge a marriage that flourishes."

— Brett Brandewie, Family Pastor at First Baptist Church Hendersonville, TN

"I had the honor of reading an early copy of this devotional & I loved every single page! Johnny & Carla are the real deal. Their marriage has weathered many storms & I so appreciate their candor & wise words. A must read for anyone struggling to understand their spouse. This book will be a gift to all who choose to open it - thank you, Johnny & Carla!"

— Jodi Sappe, J Sappe Christian Counseling and co-founder of Cross Roads Recovery

"Solidly biblical, intensely practical, and filled with wisdom born of their own decades-long marriage (forged in the fire and flourishing today), Carla and Johnny Morton have given us a splendid resource that will benefit couples all along the marriage journey. It's a tool pastors will want to use personally and recommend often!"

– Dr. Tim McCoy, Senior Pastor at Ingleside Baptist Church Macon, GA

"Marriage is precious, fragile, and seemingly under attack from all directions. Couples go into their own marriages blinded by love and believing they'll be the exception to culture's influence and the world's dangers. Unfortunately, without purposeful intention to protect this sacred covenant, the odds are not in your favor. That is why I am so thankful to Carla and Johnny Morton, founders of No Regretz Ministries, for writing this book. What you have here is a substantive, Scripture-based, story-driven resource that reminds you of the beauty and significance of marriage and how it reflects God Himself. Couples will find 52 devotions to complete together or individually that will lead them in the fundamentals of a faith-filled marriage."

– Robin Dance, life plan advisor, speaker, and author of *For All Who Wander*

Johnny & Carla Morton

From
You & Me
to
WE

A 52-Week Marriage Devotional

ISBN: 979-8-9903774-0-0 (paperback)
ISBN: 979-8-9903774-1-7 (ebook)

CONTENTS

INTRODUCTION

> *And we all, with unveiled face, beholding the glory of the Lord, are being transformed into the same image from one degree of glory to another. For this comes from the Lord who is the Spirit.*
>
> 2 Corinthians 3:18 ESV

When the Bible was written, factories did not exist. A blacksmith would use a forge to create tools, utensils, and even weapons. Forging is the process of shaping metal, usually iron during biblical times, into the desired product. By a process of heating, hammering, and quenching the iron, the blacksmith would carefully create his piece. He had to use the right amount of heat, and hammer the metal in exactly the right place with just the right amount of force. If any of these procedures were not followed, the finished product would not be as strong or durable as it should be.

Intense heat and pressure are also what God often uses to shape people into his trophies of grace, and marriage is often the crucible. He is the Master Blacksmith, and his heat, pressure, and touch are always perfect. First Peter 1:7 (NLV) tells us, "These tests have come to prove your faith and to show that it is good. Gold, which can be destroyed, is tested by fire. Your faith is worth much more than gold and it must be tested also. Then your faith will bring thanks and shining-greatness and honor to Jesus Christ when He comes again."

One flesh ... God says that when a man and women join in marriage, they become one (Gen. 2:24). Whether the couple choose to act as one or not, God says they are one. For years, we acted much more often as two individuals, you and me, than we did as one. There were moments we experienced the oneness of a "we", but those moments were few. It took the Master Blacksmith to forge us into one.

In our life together, both our oneness in marriage and our faith have been forged through fire. God used a variety of experiences, including our immaturity, our financial struggles, our loss of jobs, and the loss of our oldest son following heart surgery, among other things, to shape us. It took intense heat and pressure to bring us to this sweet spot in marriage, and the experience has not been anything we expected, planned for, or at times wanted. We have grown exponentially, however, and our passion now is to help couples forge a marriage that will flourish in all seasons and learn to live as one.

We have designed this devotional book to be used weekly for a year. Even if one spouse does not want to participate, the other will no doubt find valuable resources to employ. The topics covered will span the breadth of marriage issues, helping you improve your marriage through God's guidance from his Word and weekly challenges that we have used.

We pray that God will use this as a tool to help your marriage flourish. Keep on Forging!

Carla & Johnny Morton
No Regretz Ministries, 2024

WEEK 1

UNDERSTANDING THE "WHY"

> *God said, "It's not good for the Man to be alone; I'll make him a helper, a companion." God put the Man into a deep sleep. As he slept, he removed one of his ribs and replaced it with flesh. God then used the rib that he had taken from the Man to make Woman and presented her to the Man.*
>
> Genesis 2:18, 21–22 MSG

We believe that understanding the "why" of marriage is foundational. If we do not understand God's purposes in marriage, if we miss the big picture, it is so easy to either settle, give up, or get out.

Marriage is the relationship designed by God, patterned after the relationship of the Trinity, whereby God joins together a man and a woman into one flesh. It is designed to fulfill our longing for companionship, intimacy, and vulnerability, as well as to raise godly generations. Marriage creates a partnership that God uses to mold us into the image of Christ, teaching us to love our spouse and others with a selfless love so we may display to the world the glorious truth of the gospel—that God loves us in our brokenness, Jesus died to redeem us, and God desires an intimate relationship with us.

Let's look at some of the key truths from the definition above. We will look at these truths in more detail in the days ahead.

- Because we are created in God's image (Genesis 1:27), we are created for relationship with him and with others. We are not meant to live life alone.

- God created marriage (Genesis 2:24). Following his principles for it leads to the healthiest marriages.

- While only God can meet our deepest needs as we lean into him, he uses us to meet the needs of our spouse (Phil. 4:19).

- God calls us to raise godly generations (Deut. 6:7).

- God uses marriage to mold us into the image of Christ. Our flaws and weaknesses will be revealed (Romans 8:29).

- God's design is that marriage be a living portrait of the gospel (Eph. 5:21-33).

We need to understand that God's design for marriage is much more amazing than most people realize. Marriage is a key part of his plan to reconcile the world to himself, for when we marry, we play a unique role in God's story. God has a part for you in his story that only the two of you can fulfill together. As you begin this journey, from whatever place you are in your marriage, be ready for God to do more than you can imagine!

> The Man said, "Finally! Bone of my bone, flesh of my flesh! Name her Woman for she was made from Man." Therefore, a man leaves his father and mother and embraces his wife. They become one flesh. The two of them, the Man and his Wife, were naked, but they felt no shame. (Genesis 2:23–25 MSG)

COUPLES ♥ CHALLENGE

♥ *Discuss with your spouse why each of you wanted to be married.*

♥ *Answer these questions: Are your reasons for marrying the same as God's reasons for marriage? What is similar? What is different?*

♥ *Pray that God will use this book to transform your lives individually and your marriage.*

WEEK 2

IMAGO DEI

> *Then God said, "Let Us (Father, Son, Holy Spirit) make man in Our image, according to Our likeness [not physical, but a spiritual personality and moral likeness]; and let them have complete authority over the fish of the sea, the birds of the air, the cattle, and over the entire earth, and over everything that creeps and crawls on the earth." So God created man in His own image, in the image and likeness of God He created him; male and female He created them.*
>
> **Genesis 1:26–27 AMP**

As human beings, we are distinct from everything else God created because only we were created in *imago Dei*, the image of God. So, how should the fact that we are image bearers

7

impact our marriages? Let's consider what it means to be created *imago Dei* and the influence that should have in our marriages.

- Because God is relational, we are created to be in relationships with others. Notice that Scripture says "Let us make man in *Our* likeness." The Trinity is a relationship between the Father, the Son, and the Holy Spirit. They love each other. I know it's hard to wrap our minds around the concept of the Trinity, but that love relationship is the basis for all human relationships. God designed us for relationship.

- God gives us the ability to think and reason. We are not simply creatures of instinct and appetite. We can apply knowledge and reasoning to live our lives. We can choose to intentionally apply God's principles to our marriage.

- We have moral freedom. We can choose obedience or disobedience. We can choose to do good or evil. This also means we are responsible for the choices we make. We choose to love our spouse or not, but we are responsible for that choice.

- We can live transcendent lives. We can live for something bigger than just ourselves. We can live for God's glory, and we can also live our lives for the benefit of others. In marriage, we can choose to put our spouse and their needs ahead of our own. We can love as Christ did and put others first.

So, what does all this mean for our marriages? God created marriage. We can choose to marry or not. If we choose to marry, God has given us principles to live by and the ability to apply those principles to our unique marriage relationship. The way we do it may not be the way another couple does it. In fact, that is the design. Great marriages take work, intentionality, and our choice to cooperate with God in the process.

Choose wisely!

> God's power has given us everything we need for life and godliness, through our knowing the One who called us to his own glory and goodness. (2 Peter 1:3 CJB)

COUPLES ♥ CHALLENGE

♥ How does it make you feel to know that you have been created in God's image? Encouraged? Challenged? Something else? Discuss with your spouse.

♥ Of the four aspects of imago Dei, which one resonates with you the most? Why?

♥ What are specific ways that your marriage can image God at home? At work? With your friends?

PARADISE LOST

> *When the woman saw that the fruit was good*
> *for food, and pleasing to the eye, and desirable*
> *for gaining wisdom, she took some and ate it.*
> *She also gave some to her husband, who was*
> *with her, and he ate it.*
>
> **Genesis 3:6 NIV**

The first time in Scripture when God said something was not good was when he declared it was not good for Adam to be alone. Adam had named all the animals, but no suitable helpmate was found in that group. God then created Eve out of Adam and brought her to him. It's fun to imagine what that must have been like for Adam to wake up, missing a rib, and there was a woman just for him!

Adam said, "Now, this is bone of my bone, and flesh of my flesh; she shall be called woman for she was taken out of man" (Genesis 2:23 ESV). He recognized that Eve was like him in many ways and yet so different. She was the perfect helpmate.

The word *helpmate* has two parts:

- *Kenegdo*, which means opposite, counterpart, alongside.
- *Ezer*, which is more difficult to translate, but at its root refers to the idea of being strong, rescuing, and saving.

The word *helpmate* is used twenty-one times in the Old Testament. The first time was to describe the woman, while most of the other times it was used as a military term.

At the end of Genesis 2, Adam and his wife were both naked and felt no shame. Wow! What an incredible mindset. Total unveiled exposure in every way, with perfect unity.

We know what happened next. Satan tempted Eve. He made her question what God had really said. He caused her to look at the fruit from the tree in the middle of the garden and decide that not only did it look good for food and look pleasing to the eye, *but* it could also give her wisdom. She likely wondered, *Could God be holding out on us?* At the root of this first sin, like all sins, Eve decided that she could choose her own way and find fulfillment outside of God. She took the fruit, ate it, and then gave some to Adam to eat. He was with her but did nothing to stop her, and acquiesced when she gave it to him.

At this moment, sin entered the world; perfection was shattered. Immediately their eyes were opened and they realized they were naked. They felt exposed and vulnerable. They sewed fig leaves to cover themselves.

The minute they sinned, their relationship with God was broken. They had disobeyed God. As well, their relationship with each other was fractured. Vertical, then horizontal damage ensued. In that moment they lost their perfect unity and total delight in each other.

After covering themselves, they hid. We spend our lives trying to cover what we don't want others to see. They hid from God, as if God could not find them. When God asked them why they were hiding, Adam said, "I was naked and afraid" (Genesis 3:10 ESV). The exposure they now had before God, due to their broken relationship, made them feel afraid.

When God confronted them about what they had done, they started the blame game. Adam passively blamed God by saying, "The woman whom you gave to be with me, she gave me fruit of the tree, and I ate" (Genesis 3:12 ESV). Eve blamed the serpent, Satan, for deceiving her. So, now we live in a fallen world with the consequences of our fallen nature and our sinful choices.

But the good news is that as believers in Jesus Christ, we have a way back to the Father. We can have our relationship with God restored because of Jesus's sacrificial death that paid the price for our sin. We can now be in right relationship with God, and we can also redeem what God intends for our marriage relationships. It will not be perfect this side of heaven, but it can be glorious.

> For all have sinned, and fall short of the glory of God, and all are justified freely by his grace through the redemption that came by Christ Jesus. (Romans 3:23 NIV)

> Blessed are those whose transgressions are forgiven, whose sins are covered. Blessed is the one whose sin the Lord will never count against them. (Romans 4:7–8 NIV)

COUPLES ♥ CHALLENGE

♥ Talk about what you imagine Adam must have thought when he saw Eve. Husbands, describe what you thought when you saw your bride for the first time on your wedding day.

♥ Eve would never have been compared to any other woman by Adam. Wives, what do you think that would have felt like?

♥ Tell your spouse what being totally unveiled but safe might be like for you.

♥ When you think about Adam and Eve living perfectly with each other, what is one thing you want to have of that experience with in your marriage?

WEEK 4

A DOUBLE-EDGED
SWORD

Do nothing out of selfish ambition or vain conceit.
Rather, in humility value others above yourselves,
not looking to your own interests but each of you
to the interest of the other.

Philippians 2:3–4 NIV

Hebrews 4:12 tells us that God's Word, the Bible, is "sharper than any two-edged sword, piercing to the division of soul and of spirit, of joints and of marrow, and discerning the thoughts and intentions of the heart" (ESV). Marriage for believers is like a double-edged sword, meaning there are two major aspects. On one edge is the opportunity to experience the restoration of what was lost in the fall. On the other edge is how God uses marriage to sanctify us, to cut away all that is unlike Jesus. We can learn to enjoy our spouse, and we can learn to cherish what God intended when he made us different but designed us complementary. We can move toward unity, an increasing intimacy on all levels, and can experience some of the wonders of the garden.

One of the ways we learn to do this is by acknowledging that God created this thing called marriage. He knows how he designed it to work, and it will only work well when we follow his pattern. God gave us each different roles, perspectives, gifts, strengths, and weaknesses. When we learn to accept and celebrate our differences, we can start to embrace the wonder of how God designed marriage to work.

In marriage we have someone to help us, to partner with us for the journey of this life. We are to cleave to each other, bear one another's burdens, and experience the wonder of being seen and loved in the most intimate ways.

God's desire is that we reclaim what was lost in the fall and learn to flourish in our relationship. He desires that we learn to cherish our spouse to see them as they truly are, the lovely and the unlovely, growing in appreciation and honor of the unique person they are, while encouraging them to be the best version of themselves. It is noticing and celebrating the excellence you see in them to all around you. It is guarding and protecting them from anything that might harm them or your relationship.

This one edge of restoring God's divine purpose for marriage is still a struggle if we fight against God's intentions. If we can only see our perspective and our way, or if we only focus on what our spouse lacks, then we miss seeing how our strengths can balance our weaknesses and how we are stronger together than apart.

We must choose to want this for our marriage. It does not happen automatically. It is an intentional day-in-and-day-out decision to pour into our marriage so we can enjoy the fruit of God's plan.

That is why a man leaves his father and mother and is united to his wife, and they become one flesh. Adam and his wife were both naked, and they felt no shame. (Genesis 2:24–25 NIV)

Be devoted to one another in love. Honor one another above yourselves. (Romans 12:10 NIV)

COUPLES ♥ CHALLENGE

♥ Each of you share a strength that you admire in your spouse.

♥ Does your spouse's strength balance a weakness you have?

♥ What does the word **cherish** mean to you? Make sure you understand your spouse's definition.

♥ Share one way you would like to be cherished. Be specific.

♥ Ask each other this question: When was a time when you really felt cherished, honored, appreciated, and loved? Why did you feel that way?

THE CUTTING EDGE

For those God foreknew he also predestined to be conformed to the image of his Son, that He might be the firstborn among many brothers and sisters.

Romans 8:29 NIV

I (Carla) was introduced to this other edge of the sword years ago when we went for counseling. Now, I was certain Johnny was the issue. He would not do what I wanted him to do! I was totally frustrated. This marriage was not what I'd signed on for. So can you imagine my shock when after I carefully explained the situation, the counselor looked at me and said, "Carla, this issue is not about Johnny." Are you kidding me? This started my long process in understanding what God was doing.

This edge of the sword is unique to believers. It is where we see God's other purpose in our marriage. God's plan from eternity past has been that marriage would reflect the relationship between Christ and his church. In the Old Testament, this had not yet been revealed. In Ephesians 5 we see this mystery disclosed—that our marriage relationships go beyond what occurred in the garden of Eden.

Marriage between believers has a high and holy calling. Our marriages have eternal purposes. This means that God will use our marriages, as much as anything else in this life, to sanctify us. Our marriages reveal the real us. We can hide or cover up from others, but in marriage we are exposed. It is like a big mirror, showing all our flaws. God will use our marriages and his truth to change us, teach us, humble us, and give us a place where we learn to sacrificially love someone else.

This is part of the reason that marriage is hard. Yes, if we are believers we are saved, but we still sin. We still struggle in many ways. We need not be surprised by the depth of God's work in and through our marriages. If we can firmly grasp that part of God's intention in marriage is to use it to transform us, then it helps us see the big picture. For believers, it can help us not grow weary, and not lose sight of God's eternal purpose in our marriage. It helps us not to give up when things get tough, because many times it may be hard. I struggled for years to understand this, but it was so freeing when I did.

Marriage is a training ground for learning to forgive, extend grace, redeem our mistakes, and demonstrate reconciliation. Therefore, it is imperative that believers understand that marriage is like a sword. It has two edges. Yes, we get to redeem what was lost in the fall. But the other side is that we understand God's eternal purpose. Marriage is to reflect the relationship of Christ and his church. We model this to the world. The mystery of Christ loving his church, represented in a husband loving his wife, gives our marriages a new high and holy calling.

It is God's will that you should be sanctified. (1 Thessalonians 4:3 NIV)

For the word of God is alive and powerful. It is sharper than the sharpest two-edged sword, cutting between soul and spirit, between joint and marrow. It exposes our innermost thoughts and desires. (Hebrews 4:12 NLT)

COUPLES ♥ CHALLENGE

♥ *Share with your spouse what has been one thing in your marriage God has used to teach you something or change something about yourself.*

♥ *What is one way you love yourself? How might you love your spouse in the same way or similarly?*

♥ *How would you rate this statement: "If marriage is too hard, we must be doing something wrong"?*

   1 = True

   2 = Some truth

   3 = Not certain

   4 = Maybe false

   5 = False

♥ *Discuss the following excerpt, considering your answer above:*

> *"This is part of the reason that marriage is hard.*
> *Yes, if we are believers we are saved, but we still*
> *sin. We still struggle in many ways. We need not be*
> *surprised by the depth of God's work in and through*
> *our marriage. If we can firmly grasp that part of God's*
> *intention in marriage is to use it to transform us,*
> *then it helps us see the big picture."*

RAISING A GODLY GENERATION

"Listen, O Israel! The LORD is our God, the LORD alone. And you must love the LORD your God with all your heart, all your soul, and all your strength. And you must commit yourselves wholeheartedly to these commands that I am giving you today. Repeat them again and again to your children. Talk about them when you are at home and when you are on the road, when you are going to bed and when you are getting up. Tie them to your hands and wear them on your forehead as reminders. Write them on the doorposts of your house and on your gates."

Deuteronomy 6:4–9 NLT

After God created Adam and Eve, he gave them a three-part mandate. The first was to be fruitful and multiply. From the beginning, God's plan to populate his world was through the marriage of a husband and wife and the children they would bear. So, while the husband/wife relationship is the priority in marriage, marriage is also about the generations that spring from that relationship. Here is a simple question: What should our primary goal be in raising children?

Being a Christian parent today and trying to follow the principles of the Bible in raising children is going to be a challenge. You will find yourselves swimming upstream against the culture. You may feel like giving up as your child tests you again and again. We know parenting well is hard to do.

I remember when our middle child was in middle school and went to a movie with some friends—a movie that I had told him he could not go to. I had a choice to make. I could wait and talk with him later or I could do something a little more radical. I chose the second option.

I went to the movie theater, found him sitting with his friends, and told him I had to talk to him outside. I knew he was going to be mad, perhaps embarrassed, but it was important for him to learn. I'm sure he did not like me for a while afterward. That's okay. My main calling is to be his parent, not his friend. Again, it's not easy to be a parent. So, what should our focus be in raising our children according to Scripture?

For some, the goal is to raise happy children. Sounds good. Yes, I want my kids to be happy, but at what cost? If the idea is to do whatever it takes to make our children happy, we are in for long years. If happiness means giving our children whatever they want, we do them a disservice. We need to prepare them for disappointment because they will face their share of it as they make their way in a fallen world.

For other parents, the goal is to raise successful children. We want to give them every chance to succeed at whatever they do. To that end we sign them up for every sport or other activity. We run them from soccer to gymnastics and then to piano so they can find what they excel at doing. We push them to be excellent in everything they do, so if they're struggling, we let them quit or bail them out. We run interference for them so they never have to experience failure. Instead of successful young adults who can learn and overcome disappointments, we end up with entitled adolescents who believe that the worst thing in life is failure.

It may seem like we are against children being happy and successful. Of course we aren't. The key is not making success or happiness the goal. The goal is to raise godly children—to teach them to love and glorify God. We want them to understand that the world does not revolve around them. We want them to learn to handle disappointment and failure, as they are some of God's greatest teaching tools. We teach them to love God and serve others. We teach them that God will supply their needs and he is always good, even if their circumstances are hard. Make it your goal to raise godly children, and they can help change the world.

COUPLES ♥ CHALLENGE

♥ *What is your goal for raising your children? Does your spouse feel the same? Talk about it together.*

♥ *How do you and your spouse line up when it comes to the discipline, education, extracurricular activities, and spiritual formation of your children? Where do you agree? Are there areas where you disagree with each other? Discuss any differences you have.*

♥ *Are your beliefs and principles about raising children in line with the Bible? Your friends? The culture? Discuss with your spouse.*

♥ *This is a key area to work on together and be on the same page. Work out any differences you and your spouse have so that you are supporting each other.*

WEEK 7

THE MYSTERY OF MARRIAGE

As the Scriptures say, "A man leaves his father and mother and is joined to his wife, and the two are united into one." This is a great mystery, but it is an illustration of the way Christ and the church are one.

Ephesians 5:31–32 NLT

I (Johnny) don't know about you, but I love a good mystery. Whether a good book or a movie, mystery is one of my favorite genres. I love trying to figure out what happened and who did what. The best mysteries are the ones that keep you guessing until the very end.

The Bible has mysteries. Some of them are beyond our comprehension, such as the Trinity. We can study it, read commentaries, and wrestle with the concept until we are mentally exhausted, but in the end, our minds just can't totally fathom it. But then, there are other mysteries found in Scripture. Things that were confounding in the Old Testament but on the other side of the cross have been revealed in the New Testament. Things that were shadows in the Old Testament but are now made clear in the New. The mystery of the gentiles becoming a part of the church, to which Paul alludes in Colossians 1:27, is one example. The mystery of marriage is another.

Of all the purposes of marriage, the mystery of it is the pinnacle. It doesn't mean the other purposes of marriage we considered in the preceding weeks are unimportant, but the highest purpose is revealed in the mystery of marriage, as Paul reveals in Ephesians 5. The unity of a man and woman in marriage is designed to reflect God's relationship with his people. In the Old Testament, Israel is seen in a marriage relationship with God. In the New Testament, Jesus is the bridegroom and the church is his bride. Marriage is meant to put the gospel on display for all the world to see, "teaching us to love our spouse and others with a selfless love so we may display to the world the glorious truth of the gospel—that God loves us in our brokenness, Jesus died to redeem us, and God desires an intimate relationship with us!" (Week 1 reading).

What a high calling! Marriage is far more than a relationship to meet our needs or a place to raise godly generations, as important as those purposes are. Marriage is a jewel to be put on display before the world so that God's unconditional love, sacrifice, and commitment to his children may be seen in the relationship between a husband and wife as they exhibit the same in their marriage. Marriage is designed to be a vital part in revealing God to the culture we live in. If we understand that truth, all the other purposes become clearer.

So, the question we must ask ourselves is this: What do others see when they look at my marriage? Do they see unconditional, self-sacrificing love and commitment to each other, or do they see something less than that? We strive for those things not just because we have a more fulfilling marriage, but because it will bring much glory to God.

> Well, whatever you do, whether it's eating or drinking or anything else, do it all so as to bring glory to God. (1 Corinthians 10:31 CJB)

COUPLES ♥ CHALLENGE

♥ *What do you think people see when they look at your marriage? Why do you think they see that?*

♥ *How does the concept that your marriage is meant to reflect God's relationship to his people make you feel? Excited? Fearful? Challenged? Share your feelings and discuss why you feel that way.*

♥ *How could your marriage better reflect God's relationship to his people? What steps do you need to take to ensure that happens?*

WHERE DO WE GO FROM HERE?

> *You shall know the truth, and the truth shall set you free.*
>
> **John 8:32 NIV**

Maybe you have read the first several devotionals and are thinking, *Well, we are not there*, or *We sure have messed up*. Haven't we all! In some ways, when we started out in our marriage, I (Carla) thought I knew some things, but really I didn't. I wrongly assumed that because we were both believers and were in ministry, certainly things would go well. The reality was that marriage was so much harder than I expected. Our marriage was like living on the cutting edge of the sword. It was the iron sharpening iron removing the rough places. I really didn't understand it at that time. I struggled against it, fighting God at every turn.

Maybe this is where you find yourself: marriage is more challenging than you thought, requires more of you than you want to give up at times, and doesn't always feel good. So where do you go from here?

I think the first thing we must do is align our mind with the truth. Acknowledge that God will use your marriage to change you. He will use things about your spouse to challenge and confront you. God will grow and mature you in and through your marriage.

One of the most freeing things that happened to me was understanding that God would use my marriage to do far more than I could imagine. God will use the places that are hard in your marriage to reveal things to you about yourself, your relationship to him, and what you have believed. God had much he needed to teach me. What's amazing is that when I began to understand this, it became so freeing. False beliefs are bondage. Truth does set us free.

If you are just starting out, this is awesome, because you can set your mind on this truth right from the start. If you have been married for a while and are struggling, examine what you have believed. You may need to reset your mind and be willing to embrace the truth that God is doing a work. This truth doesn't mean that you won't feel the heat or the sharpening, but that you can have confidence that God is doing a work even when it is hard. This soul-felt confidence gives us endurance to continue, to stay the course and not miss what God is doing.

> Being confident of this, that He who began a good work in you will carry it on to completion, until the day of Christ Jesus. (Philippians 1:6 NIV)

Pray that your love may abound more and more in knowledge and depth of insight, so that you may be able to discern what is best and may be pure and blameless for the day of Christ. (Philippians 1:9–10 NIV)

COUPLES ♥ CHALLENGE

♥ *What is your mindset concerning your marriage? Do you see it as a place where God is working in you? Share one aspect of your relationship where God is using your spouse, like iron, to sharpen you.*

♥ *Explain why you think this sharpening process is hard for you.*

♥ *Start a marriage journal/notebook. Write down what you think God is teaching you through the struggle.*

♥ *Go back to your journal writings after two to three months to see if any change has happened. Sometimes our hearts are changing but we don't realize it. Revisiting what our struggle was and seeing change can be encouraging.*

WEEK 9

INTIMACY IN MARRIAGE

*O LORD, you have searched me and known me!
You know when I sit down and when I rise up; you
discern my thoughts from afar. You search out my
path and my lying down and are acquainted with
all my ways. Even before a word is on my tongue,
behold, O LORD, you know it altogether.*

Psalm 139:1–4 ESV

Have you ever seen a couple who seemed to be connected in a unique way? They appeared to know what the other was thinking, even finishing each other's sentences. They were comfortable with each other, loving each other passionately while totally aware of the faults and shortcomings they each had.

My (Johnny's) parents were that way. They had disagreements and conflicts, but never enough to break the connection they had. They had a deep intimacy born from doing life together for more than sixty years. After my mom passed, as we were cleaning out the attic, I came across letters they had written to each other throughout their separation during World War II. Reading them, I realized their intimacy began years before as they shared themselves completely in the pages of those letters. I envy them. We don't write letters like that anymore. Yet, we can still learn how to build an intimate marriage.

Intimacy is that deep knowing of another person. Psalm 139 talks about God's intimacy with us. He knows everything about us. The good and bad; the lovely and unlovely. He knows everything. Nothing about us is hidden from him. Because marriage is patterned after God's relationship with his people, intimacy is God's design for marriage as well.

Genesis 2:25 is evidence of the intimacy Adam and Eve shared. Nothing was hidden from the other, as attested by their unashamed nakedness. The intimacy they shared with each other was shattered by the fall. Even today, husbands and wives struggle to bring that level of intimacy back to the marriage relationship.

We each have a deep longing to be completely unveiled and known by another person. We want someone who sees us as we are—all our imperfections—and chooses us anyway. We want to be valued. We want someone we can count on to be there in all situations. We want someone with whom to share our fears and dreams. We want someone to love us even when we seem unlovable. We long for someone to partner with us in all of life's ups and downs. We want intimacy with someone else spiritually, emotionally, experientially, and physically. That's one of the reasons God created marriage—so we could find that intimacy we crave with someone.

Before we look at how to build intimacy in different areas, let's consider some of the barriers that keep us from building it in our marriage. Deep intimacy can come when we feel that our marriage is a place of safety and refuge. Several behaviors and attitudes can keep that from happening.

There are three big enemies of intimacy in marriage. The first is pride. Pride comes in several guises. One is the pride that says, "I don't need anything." We become an island unto ourselves in the marriage. This pride keeps us from recognizing our need for intimacy. The other is the pride that makes us unable to admit our fears, weaknesses, or failures to our spouse. Whether out of fear of looking less than perfect or, more likely, a fear our spouse won't love us, we hold back from opening up. A part of us always remains hidden.

A second enemy of intimacy is selfishness. Building intimacy in marriage takes both parties unveiling themselves. Selfishness leads us to hold back from giving of ourselves. We want to take from the other and not give anything in return. Selfishness can also become manipulative. We give to our spouse only if we get what we want and on our terms.

The final enemy of intimacy is much more subtle—the enemy of busyness. This often happens when we stop being intentional about our marriage relationship. As we'll see again in Week 37, we find ourselves so over-scheduled doing "good" things, even in the church, that we lose sight of what is most important. Our relationship with God, followed by our relationship with our spouse, should take precedence. When those things take a backseat to the tyranny of the urgent, we start to drift as a couple. Some stay in that place throughout the years of raising children only to find out they are living with a stranger when the children leave home. Maybe it's time to slow down and focus on the most important things.

God designed us for intimate relationship. First with him and then with another person in the relationship of marriage. Somewhere we can be fully known and fully loved. Are you growing in intimacy? Is your marriage a haven where you can be unveiled before each other? Are there barriers keeping you from experiencing God's best for your relationship? If so, it's time to do something about that.

> And the man and his wife were both naked and were not ashamed. (Genesis 2:25 ESV)

COUPLES ♥ CHALLENGE

♥ On a scale of 1–10, with 10 being the highest, where would you each put your level of intimacy in the marriage? Discuss why you chose the number you chose.

♥ Do you believe that one spouse is more unveiled than the other? If so, how does that make you feel?

♥ Are any of the barriers we looked at an issue in the relationship? Which ones? How can you remove those barriers?

♥ When was the last time you wrote a love letter? Write one to your spouse over the next few weeks telling them the ways and the whys of your love for them.

EMOTIONAL AND EXPERIENTIAL INTIMACY

So being affectionately desirous of you, we were willing to have imparted unto you, not the gospel of God only, but also our own souls, because you were dear unto us.

I Thessalonians 2:8 KJ21

Emotional intimacy is the connection we have with our spouse when we feel seen, known, and deeply valued. It is achieved when we feel safe and secure enough with our spouse that we can share our hopes, dreams, feelings, fears, opinions, likes, and dislikes. We know we will be listened to and accepted whether our spouse agrees or even understands us completely. We open ourselves up to one another, making ourselves vulnerable, and that vulnerability is essential to building emotional intimacy. As you each share the deepest parts of yourself and in turn actively listen to each other, know those moments are the seeds of deep emotional intimacy.

Here are some ways you can build emotional intimacy:

- Seek to know what is going on with your spouse. Ask open-ended questions to prevent one-word answers.

- Listen well. Focus on the speaker and remove distractions like your phone or TV.

- Don't judge or criticize your spouse. Accept and validate their views even if you don't agree with them.

- Spend time remembering your past struggles and victories. Remember when …

- Be open about everything that impacts your marriage or family. Your spouse should not be surprised about something you know but have not shared. (Some work issues may need to be confidential.)

Another type of intimacy in marriage is experiential intimacy. In marriage we are meant to do life together. Shared experiences can help bind us to each other. For men, this is often one of the strongest bonding agents. Men tend to build relationships with others by doing things together. The shared history of experiences can create deep intimacy, and this includes both good and bad experiences.

In fact, shared trauma and tragedy can create a deep bond in a husband and wife. The shared pain is something no one else can understand in the way you as a couple experienced it. Losing our oldest son, Zach, when he was eighteen has been the most traumatic moment of our lives, yet we share that tragedy in a way that creates deep intimacy.

God tells us that he uses all things to transform us, and I believe he can use all things we experience as a couple to grow deep intimacy. Both the fun times and the hard times can bind us as we share them together. Use these experiences of life as moments to build lasting intimacy.

> Two are better than one, because they have a good reward for their labor. For if they fall, one will lift up his companion. But woe to him who is alone when he falls, for he has no one to help him up. (Ecclesiastes 4:9–10 NKJV)

COUPLES ♥ CHALLENGE

♥ How emotionally connected to your spouse do you feel right now? Do you both feel the same way?

♥ Answer these questions about your spouse. After each of you answer, determine whether you are correct.

What is your spouse's greatest fear?

What makes your spouse happy?

How does your spouse feel loved and appreciated?

What is your spouse's dream?

♥ *What are some of the key experiences you have shared together, whether good or bad? Each of you make a list and then compare them. How do they connect you?*

♥ *Take a few minutes and remember these experiences together. If you are in a hard place, reflect on the hard places you have been before. Use them to encourage you now.*

♥ *Give thanks for how God has used those experiences to mold you and your marriage.*

PHYSICAL AND SPIRITUAL INTIMACY

Then the man said, "This at last is bone of my bones and flesh of my flesh; she shall be called Woman, because she was taken out of Man." Therefore, a man shall leave his father and his mother and hold fast to his wife, and they shall become one flesh.

Genesis 2:23–24 ESV

Let's get this out of the way. Physical intimacy is not just about sex. Sorry, guys. Now, sex is a part of physical intimacy in marriage, but physical intimacy is so much more. Another key point—the presence or lack of physical intimacy often reflects the depth of intimacy in the other areas. If you don't feel emotionally or spiritually intimate with your spouse, that tends to impact the physical intimacy as well. Remember, intimacy grows as you feel safe, secure, seen, and heard in your marriage. When that is lacking, you really might get (or give) the cold shoulder. If you see the desire for physical intimacy is waning, look at the other aspects of intimacy in your marriage. How deep are they?

Physical intimacy is all about those physical touches that communicate being seen, understood, and cherished. It is the hug and kiss when you have not been together. It is holding hands as you walk from your car to your destination. It is cuddling on the couch. It is the subtle touches when you are in public that say, "You are mine, and I am here for you."

Our brains are wired with a need for physical touch, and each time we touch our spouse in a loving, caring way it can build the connection between us. Yes, sex is a part, but these other physical touches are just as important. Don't neglect them. We will look at sexual intimacy later in this book, but for now, let's look at the crown jewel of intimacy: spiritual intimacy.

Spiritual intimacy begins with the Trinity. The Father, the Son, and the Holy Spirit are in a loving relationship in the Godhead. Because we are created in God's image, we are made for relationship with God and with each other. The relationship of marriage is the union of two persons into one unity. We are separate, unique individuals joined as one by God. Even though we may have different temperaments, different gifts, different ways of connecting to God, and profoundly different ways of thinking, spiritual oneness, or spiritual intimacy, arises from these differences fitting together.

So, what is spiritual intimacy? It is a sense of unity and mutual commitment to God's purpose for our lives and marriage. It is the power of the Holy Spirit being experienced and released in our relationship as we open our hearts to each other and to the

Lord. As a product of a Christ-centered marriage, it can only be experienced by two Christians. The diagram below shows how, as we pursue our relationship with Christ individually, we grow into a deep spiritual intimacy together.

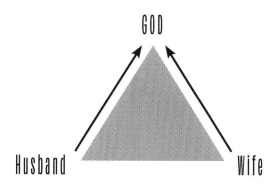

Spiritual intimacy is not

- Connecting to God in the same way as your spouse.

- Praying and studying the Bible together every day.

- Having an absence of conflict in your marriage. (Spiritually intimate couples still have conflicts. They just handle that conflict in healthy ways.)

The marks of a spiritually intimate marriage include

- A consistent prayer life praying for your spouse and your marriage.

- Suffering together and being redeemed together.

- Honoring and respecting each other in conflict.

- A willingness to risk more for your spouse, including making yourself vulnerable to them in all aspects of your life.

- Pursuing the kingdom of God separately and together.

In the part of God's amazing story of redeeming a broken world through Jesus, marriage has a unique role by demonstrating to the world God's love and redemption as a husband and wife pursue God together. Your own relationship with God is key to building spiritual intimacy as a couple. Deep intimacy, trust, and love are found at the foot of the cross.

> Then God said, "Let us make man in our image, after our likeness." (Genesis 1:26 ESV)

COUPLES ♥ CHALLENGE

♥ *Answer these questions:*

> *What types of non-sexual touches make you feel loved?*
>
> *Do you want more or fewer physical touches outside of sex?*
>
> *Do either of you avoid physical intimacy when you don't feel connected in other areas?*

♥ *Try some of these tips to build spiritual intimacy in the coming weeks:*

> *Share what God has been teaching you over the past weeks.*
>
> *Pick a book on either marriage or spiritual growth to read together. Set a schedule of each of you reading one devotional a week and then discussing it.*
>
> *Find a place to serve together.*
>
> *If you are not in a small group as a couple, find one to try out together.*
>
> *Find a marriage retreat or conference and sign up for it.*

♥ *Take an online assessment based on "Sacred Pathways: Discover Your Soul's Path to God" by Gary Thomas © 1996.*
https://form.jotform.com/221393702575053

WEEK 12

WHEN TRUST IS BROKEN

The heart of her husband trusts in her, and
he will have no lack of gain.

Proverbs 31:11 NIV

One of the issues we struggled with in our marriage was broken trust. When dealing with financial issues we were having, Johnny decided not to tell me (Carla) the extent of the issue out of the misguided notion of "protecting" me. (I think he actually wanted to protect himself from me.) This broke my trust in him when he didn't tell me the whole truth, and it took several months before I felt that I could trust him again.

Trust is the glue that binds a husband and wife together. It means "I know you have my back, you are on my side, you are open with me, you will be honest with me, and you will protect and defend us. I am safe with you." When Johnny wasn't completely open with me, I felt unsafe.

Trust can be broken in dozens of ways in a marriage relationship, and either spouse can break trust. Some offenses may have lesser consequences than others, but every broken trust has the potential to create harm and damage the relationship. The offense does not have to be horrific (based on your definition) to cause pain for your spouse.

Trust is like a bungee cord. The cord can bind, secure, and safeguard. If the bungee cord is tying us together but one of us lets go, that cord will go flying at the other one. They will feel the sting as the cord snaps them. That is a picture of what happens when trust is broken. The sting is real, and the disappointment can be crushing. If the cord has snapped, it is not binding us.

When trust has been broken, it must be repaired for the relationship to be able to mend and move forward. So, where do we start? The beginning is an honest confession. This can be painful, hard, and totally uncomfortable. But it is critical. The spouse that has broken trust can't act as if it hasn't happened. They must not lie, downplay, excuse, or defend what occurred. (It took Johnny a while to learn this.)

Confession of the offense must be made for any healing to begin, and this applies no matter the level of the trust that was broken. Once there has been an honest confession, the wounded spouse has a choice to make. God's desire is that we forgive those who have wounded us. Forgiveness is a choice. It does not mean that the offense will be forgotten or excused. It means "I will choose not to take vengeance; I will not make you continue to 'pay.'" (If you are struggling with forgiving your spouse, check out the Week 46 devotional for a deeper look at forgiveness.)

Now, after confession and forgiveness, how do you learn to trust again? How do you reattach the bungee cord? The reconnection may be slow based on the severity of the offense. It may require exaggerated openness and vulnerability to help the wounded spouse have some level of comfort. Trust may need to be "verified," and it may require and need accountability with someone else. We may put the bungee cord back around us, but we will also need to keep checking that it is tight and secure.

Can the cord become strong and supportive again? Absolutely. Might it take time, assistance, or support from others (e.g., a counselor or accountability person)? Absolutely. Will it be worth it to repair the bungee cord and have it be stronger, tighter, and more secure than ever? Absolutely!

> For we all sin and stumble in many ways. (James 3:2 AMP)

> Bear with each other and forgive one another if any of you has a grievance against someone. Forgive as the Lord has forgiven you. (Colossians 3:13 NIV)

COUPLES ♥ CHALLENGE

♥ *Has there been a time when trust was broken in your marriage? What happened?*

♥ *Have you dealt with it? If you haven't, you need to. Create a plan with action steps.*

♥ *What boundaries may need to be in place to protect the relationship?*

♥ *Discuss the things you each need to move forward.*

MARRIAGE BY DESIGN

> *Not that I have already obtained this or am already perfect, but I press on to make it my own, because Jesus Christ has made me his own.*
>
> **Philippians 3:12 ESV**

*I*ntentionality is a word we have come to believe in and speak about all the time. The reason is this: great marriages do not just happen! Great marriages are born out of being intentional. Human nature has a bent toward drifting, taking the path of least resistance, just floating along, and the drift is never toward more intimacy or a stronger connection. The danger is that drifting takes you away from what God intended marriage to be.

Anything that is worthwhile takes intentional effort. If we want to experience the richest benefits of marriage, we must decide to intentionally pursue one another. There are several aspects to this. We will look at just a few.

♥ **Marriage as a priority**

This will look different for every couple, but your
marriage must be your top priority after your
relationship with God. It is more important than your
career and your children. Is it hard to do this? Yes!
The pull of our jobs and raising children is constant. It
requires so much of our time, but we must determine
that our marriage must be at the center. Our careers will
change and someday end. Raising children, who leave
home to establish their own homes, will end.

♥ **Developing intimacy**

Intimacy grows as you seek to know one another. It is
looking away from everything else to truly see your
spouse. This occurs when you spend time together,
whether it be having date nights, finding time after kids
are in bed, scheduling time away, or playfully connecting
during the day via texts, calls, or notes.

♥ **Shared partnership**

In marriage you must learn to recognize each other's
strengths and to balance your weaknesses. James 3:2
tells us that we all stumble and make mistakes (ESV).
We each have blind spots, areas where we can easily be
misled and fall into sin. As you partner together, you
can challenge each other but also have each other's
back. You help cover each other's "blind side." You are
joined together so that you face the world with someone
who is on your side. You are giving encouragement,
celebrating victories, sharing heartaches, and forging
ahead together.

Marriage is intended to be a place of mystical intimacy, genuine delight, and enjoyment of each other as you move together toward God. Embrace the journey.

> Look carefully then how you walk, not as unwise but as wise, making the best use of the time, because the days are evil. Therefore, do not be foolish, but understand what the will of the Lord is. (Ephesians 5:15 ESV)

> Let us consider how to spur one another on toward love and good deeds. (Hebrews 10:24 ESV)

COUPLES ♥ CHALLENGE

- ♥ *Put together a date night schedule. These dates don't have to take place every week, but what can you make happen? Start small but set a goal.*

- ♥ *Each of you write down five topics/questions and put them in a jar. Pull one out at a time for a date-night talk or the next time you are together in the car.*

- ♥ *Pick at least two times a week (select the day and time) and each of you share one good thing about your day/week and one challenging or hard thing.*

- ♥ *Repeat this process. If you set up a date night and then it didn't happen, don't be discouraged. Just reschedule it.*

CREATING A VISION FOR YOUR MARRIAGE

Trust God from the bottom of your heart; don't try to figure out everything on your own. Listen for God's voice in everything you do, everywhere you go; he's the one who will keep you on track.

Proverbs 3:5–6 MSG

Every summer we take a family vacation to the beach. At this point, there are three generations with a total of eighteen people. We set the dates, search for a house big enough to fit all eighteen of us, and then tell the family our destination. Once that is done, each part of the family makes their plans. We know the destination, but each decides how they will get there. Most of us drive, but some may have to fly. Some like the interstate, while others take the backroads. Eventually, we all show up at the same destination. The key is knowing where we are going.

What if we didn't set a destination? What if we just gave people the dates and said, "See you there"? Chaos would reign. How can you plan a trip for eighteen people and not know where you're going? But many couples seem to live their marriages like that. They set out with a vague idea of what kind of marriage they want but without a set destination in mind. We often say to couples that marriage is a journey, but like planning a family vacation, you need to clearly know where you're going.

A lot of people create a plan for their business lives; they set one-year plans, five-year plans, and so on. They create goals to help them get there. So, why do so many couples not create a vision for their marriage? They just drift through their marriage, hoping it ends up somewhere good. And then, when that five- or ten-year anniversary comes around, they realize their marriage is floundering with no direction or purpose.

If you want a great marriage, you need to be intentional about taking steps to create the marriage you want. It doesn't just happen, and it starts with sitting down together and asking, "What do we want our marriage to be?" For a Christian couple, the answer should start with Jesus's admonition in Matthew 6:33 (AMP): "But first and most importantly seek (aim at, strive after) His kingdom and His righteousness [His way of doing and being right—the attitude and character of God], and all these things will be given to you also."

As you think about what you want your marriage to be, seeking God's kingdom is your guiding principle. How you do that in your marriage is up to you. So, how do you create a vision for your marriage? Start with praying for God's wisdom and direction. Then do some self-evaluation both as individuals and as a couple. Ask these questions:

- Where are we now in our relationship?

- Where do we want to be a year from now?

- What do we want our unique marriage to be about?

Once you have a vision that you both agree on, that vision becomes your mission statement for your marriage. It makes it easier to discern opportunities that come your way. If something fits into your vision, go for it. If it doesn't, that makes it easier to say no.

Remember this: we can make plans, but God orchestrates our steps (Proverbs 16:9 ESV). Seek him together as a couple and walk in the freedom that comes from knowing a sovereign God has you in his hands. No one wants your marriage to thrive more than God does.

COUPLES ♥ CHALLENGE

Individually, take some time to answer this question: "Where do I want our marriage to be a year from now?"

Get a piece of paper and write down thoughts and words that come to mind as you think about a vision for your marriage.

When you finish, choose five or six words or phrases that capture the principles of what you want your marriage to be about.

- *Set up a date night to talk about what each of you came up with. Take turns sharing the five or six words you chose. Make sure you're both clear on what you mean for each.*

- *As a couple, choose at least four of the words or phrases that you want to set as a vision for your marriage for the coming year.*

- *Write them out as a mission statement and post it where you will both see it to remind you of what you want your marriage to be.*

THE PATH TO
THE VISION

But seek first the kingdom of God and his righteousness, and all these things will be added to you.

Matthew 6:33 ESV

Hopefully, after last week's devotional, you have been thinking about a vision for your marriage. Now the question is, how do we get there? Carla loves to set goals. She has pushed me to do the same for almost forty years. While I am not quite to her standard yet, I have learned the values of setting goals in our lives. I believe that if you are going to fulfill the vision you have created for your marriage, goals are an essential part in achieving your vision.

The Bible gives us a balanced view about setting goals. On the one hand, it extols the wisdom of planning and counting the cost (Luke 14:28). On the other hand, it warns against making goals without the guidance of God's Word and the Holy Spirit (Proverbs 3:5–6). We have our desires, but ultimately, God's sovereign desires will come to pass. If your vision for your marriage and the goals you establish seek to honor Christ, you can rest knowing that God will ultimately bring about what is good for you and his glory.

Here are some guidelines to consider as you set goals for your marriage:

- Small steps can lead to profound change. You don't often see marriages change overnight. It is the continual habits of pouring into your marriage that will produce long lasting results. So, think of small steps and changes that you can make habitual in your relationship.

- Expect the unexpected. Life happens in ways we sometimes can't anticipate. A change in your job. An unexpected pregnancy. Illness or accidents. All of these can disrupt your plans. That's okay. If you need to revise your goals or even your vision, do it. It's *your* vision, after all.

- Communicate frequently with each other about where you are in the journey. Remember you are a team. Encourage and pray for each other when things happen that can impact your goals and vision.

- Don't forget to celebrate along the way. Every small goal reached should be celebrated together. The fulfillment of your goals and the celebration create momentum as you move toward the marriage you want to build.

Remember, success goes to those who endure. Keep pressing toward the vision God has given you!

Good planning and hard work lead to prosperity, but hasty shortcuts lead to poverty. (Proverbs 21:5 NLT)

We can make our plans, but the LORD determines our steps. (Proverbs 16:9 NLT)

COUPLES ♥ CHALLENGE

♥ *Bring out the vision statement you worked on last week. Look at the terms or principles you chose for your vision. For each principle, describe what that would look like in your marriage if it were achieved. Make sure you both agree with the picture.*

♥ *Now that you have an idea of what your marriage will look like if your vision is achieved, make an honest assessment of where you are right now.*

♥ *For each area, begin to set small, reachable goals for that area. For example, if you want your marriage to be characterized by a deep spiritual intimacy, praying together is a part of that. But if you aren't praying together at all right now, it would be crazy to set a goal of praying together every day. You likely will fail, and that can lead to frustration. Instead, take the small step of praying together once a week and make that a habit.*

♥ *Agree on and write down the goals you have set. Put them in a place you will see daily to remind you of your goals.*

THE 5 QUESTIONS

> *Don't be selfish; don't try to impress others.*
> *Be humble, thinking of others as better than*
> *yourselves. Don't look out only for your own*
> *interests, but take an interest in others, too. You*
> *must have the same attitude that Christ Jesus had.*
>
> **Matthew 6:33 ESV**

We talk about how being intentional about our marriage is one of the keys to seeing it grow. Here is a great tool that I picked up from Mike Mobley at his *Before the Cross* blog.[1] We started using it ourselves and share it whenever we are coaching or teaching on marriage. It hits at the heart of a vibrant, healthy marriage, covering communication, service, prayer, passion, and showing love. It is also a great accountability tool to keep you on

---

1   https://beforethecross.com/encouragements/5-questions-ask-spouse-every-week/

your toes. Both of you should answer each question. Pick a time to go through the questions every week, and alternate until you have gone through all five. Let's get to it!

1. How did you feel loved or appreciated this past week?

This is a great question to see how you are doing in loving your spouse well. It focuses on how your spouse felt loved and appreciated, not on what you think you did. If you can't think of anything, time to evaluate. A good follow-up might be, "Where did I miss a chance to make you feel loved?" Loving your spouse the way they need to be loved is crucial.

2. How can I love you well this week?

I know answering this question may feel strange. We're not really used to telling someone how we want to be loved. Don't get caught up in the fallacy that you should not have to tell someone what you want—that if they love you, they should know. Maybe, if you have been married for thirty years, they may have learned. But even then we can learn new things about our spouse. Remember that marriage is a lifelong journey. Carla and I have been married for forty years, and we're still learning how to love each other well.

3. How can I pray for you this week?

Praying for one another is key to a strong marriage. It is also a great way to build intimacy as you open up and share some of your deepest needs. This question keeps you connected to your spouse in areas you may not be aware of, such as work situations. Plus, you are being obedient to God's command to pray for each other.

4. How can I serve or encourage you this week?

Marriage is about serving and supporting one another. The love that God calls us to is active, not just an emotion. Significantly, one of Jesus's final acts of love for the disciples before the cross was to wash their feet, a role usually performed by the lowest-level servant. Make sure you follow through with what your spouse tells you.

5. How would you like to be pursued in sex and intimacy this week?

Uncomfortable? You bet. I remember us both laughing when we first started using this question (it's Carla's favorite.) We are not used to talking about this; no one ever taught us how. Notice that the question addresses both sex and intimacy. Remember that intimacy is not just about sex. The more you feel emotionally and spiritually intimate with your spouse, the more your sexual relationship is likely to be satisfying. Have fun with this one!

Let no harmful language come from your mouth, only good words that are helpful in meeting the need, words that will benefit those who hear them. (Ephesians 4:29 CJB)

Out of respect for Christ, be courteously reverent to one another. (Ephesians 5:21 MSG)

COUPLES ♥ CHALLENGE

♥ *Simple challenge this week. Pick a day to ask the 5 Questions. Saturday or Sunday works for many couples. Start this week. Then make it a habit every week!*

HOW WE WERE LOVED

We love because he first loved us.

I John 4:19 ESV

P art of being human is that we are all affected by several influences in our lives. We each are uniquely designed in certain ways based on our genetic material, made up of trillions of cells and having DNA coding that directs every aspect of our growth and development. We are born this way; we did not do one thing to make it happen. It starts to occur the moment we are conceived.

The environment a person grows up in is another area of great impact. We are all imprinted by our unique family of origin. Again, there is not much we can do about it. We were not in charge when we were born, and we could not change or correct our experiences. How we were loved, or not loved, impacted us.

If you have come from a home where love was given and you were secure, you may feel free to give and receive love. But if you come from a home where love was not given or consistently offered, you probably have developed patterns of behavior to survive those insecure attachments. No one has perfectly secure attachments because no one is ever parented perfectly, and we all have effects and imprints that we bring into our marriage. This does impact how we love our spouse. Certainly, the more secure the family environment, the more likely the patterns are healthy.

Recently, we were in a marriage coaching session listening to the husband share about his family of origin, and we heard the pain of being told by his parents that he would never measure up, he was not smart enough, and he was not good enough. Deep in his soul that is still what he hears, but now it is whenever his wife complains, critiques, or criticizes. Guess what happens in his mind and heart? You got it. He hears "I am not smart enough, good enough. I don't measure up."

If you recognize that in your family of origin you did not receive secure, consistent, or dependable love, you want to acknowledge this. This is the first step in examining how it may affect your marriage. Many times, when we have not had secure love expressed, we may develop patterns of behavior such as being a pleaser or controller, being emotionally distant, or vacillating in how we respond to love. Every one of these patterns can make it extremely hard to connect consistently with our spouse. The other challenge is that if both spouses have come from families of insecure love, then there may be two opposite styles of behavior at play. These create a volatile type of dance that we repeat over and over, based on our imprinted patterns.

We cannot change those initial patterns of imprinting, but we can choose how we want to move forward. We can choose to set our mind on truth. God's Word is truth. What God says about us trumps our feelings, our experiences, and the behavior patterns we developed. We can choose to have God renew our mind; we can learn new patterns of behavior. We can learn to receive love from God and to love our spouse from that perfectly secure position. This will require honest evaluation and a willingness to deal with hard things, but the result can be new patterns of connecting in loving ways.

> Do not conform any longer to the pattern of this world but be transformed by the renewing of your mind. (Romans 12:2 NIV)

> Be made new in the attitude of your minds, and to put on the new self, created to be like God in true righteousness and holiness. (Ephesians 4:23 NIV)

COUPLES ♥ CHALLENGE

♥ *Share with your spouse what it was like growing up in your home. Focus on how your family handled conflict and provided encouragement or comfort to each other.*

♥ *Can you identify any patterns of behavior that you may have developed in response to the way you were loved or not loved?*

♥ *Ask your spouse what they see.*

♥ *Ask yourself,* Am I willing to get help in working through these patterns if needed? *What is your answer?*

THE FAMILY IN THE ROOM

> *Though my father and mother forsake me,*
> *the LORD will receive me.*
>
> **Psalm 27:10 ESV**

Most of us probably don't live in the same home as our parents. In centuries past this was more likely, but today most married couples live separately. But while our parents may not be under the same roof, they are present nevertheless through the influence our family of origin has on us. We bring all those influences into our marriage, though we may not realize it until we say or do something that our spouse sees as being like our mom or dad. They may hear it in the way we talk, or see it in the way we react or in patterns of our behavior.

These influences may have been good and a blessing or bad and we felt forsaken, but the point is that the influence is there. It will show up in our beliefs, thoughts, words, and behavior. We need to acknowledge their presence, whether good or bad. Then we need to evaluate the influence. Is it something that is a good, truthful, and right belief? If it is, then it may be that we want this to continue to influence us. If it is not a correct belief, then it may have led to thoughts or behaviors that we do not want to continue to influence us or our marriage moving forward.

We worked with a couple where the husband came from a family that was loud, expressive, and demonstrative about everything. The wife came from a family where no one expressed their emotions or shared their feelings, and certainly if they ever did, it was never in a loud, demonstrative way. Guess what? When the husband was upset, excited, and passionate about something, he raised his voice, he might yell, and he slammed the door. What did his wife do? She froze, she shut down, she was upset, and she couldn't stand it. Their families were present even though they were not physically in the room.

We can choose which "family" influences we allow to stay. We each probably bring some good things and some not-so-good things into our marriage from our family of origin. The good news? We choose! You as a couple decide what stays and what goes. You decide to embrace some of the influences, while others you may need to reject.

No other marriage will be just like mine or yours. Because each couple is a unique blend of two individuals coming together, no other marriage will be just like it. You need to build the marriage you want, but you will need to be wise and acknowledge that your families of origin have an impact, whether they are physically in the room or not.

> Blessed are those who find wisdom, those who gain understanding, for she is more profitable than silver and yields better return than gold. (Proverbs 3:13 ESV)

Above all else guard your heart, for everything you do flows from it. (Proverbs 4:23 ESV)

COUPLES ♥ CHALLENGE

♥ Share with each other one thing that you want to continue to influence you from your family of origin. Does your spouse agree with this?

♥ Are there things that you need to recognize are influencing you in ways you may not desire?

♥ Ask your spouse what they see as far as the influence of your family.

♥ If you think there is something, give a specific example so they can see how this may be affecting thoughts or behavior.

♥ What is one step you can take to start removing that influence? What do you want to replace it with?

I MARRIED YOU, NOT YOUR FAMILY

You shall teach them diligently to your children and shall talk of them when you sit in your house, and when you walk by the way, and when you lie down, and when you rise.

Deuteronomy 6:7 ESV

Hopefully, you recognize this title is a myth! It is not true. We do marry an individual, but we get the family also. We have already seen that our family of origin impacts us, so now let's explore how our families are part of our marriage equation.

We know that we leave our families to start a new one (Genesis 2:24), but the reality is our families are part of our marriage. What we need to examine is how we find that balance in guarding and protecting our marriage but also engaging with our families in ways that are healthy and wise. Family engagement is usually on a spectrum; it can be anything from overly engrossing and too connected to distant and disconnected. Each couple needs to evaluate this based on their unique family sets. What does a balance look like for your marriage? If one side of the family is too connected, are there ways to retain the connection but not allow it to overshadow your marriage, your unity?

We have worked with couples that feel such pressure to be at every "family" function because when they do not, they are ostracized, talked about, or belittled. This may require some hard conversations and a willingness to set boundaries no matter the consequences. Are there boundaries you can put in place that allow you to benefit from the close connection but preserve your unity as a couple? If one side is too distant with no connection, are there ways to try to establish some relationship that can benefit you and your family? This may have to be limited based on circumstances that are unhealthy, sinful, or toxic.

How to balance our families can be a huge deal in some marriages. Sometimes it may be that there is just so much connection everywhere (maybe on both sides) that you lose the two of you. Other times the pull of a family to deal with hard issues they are experiencing can be draining and damaging if you are not careful. The wise balance will take prayer, intentional discussion, and joint decisions. Every couple reading this page may experience this in a unique way, and the balance for your marriage will likely not look the same as someone else's.

God's intention is that families have a godly influence on the next generation. We can learn, grow, be challenged, and be shaped by the wisdom of our families. We also know that we live in a fallen world, and sadly our families may not be able to provide that kind of influence. As a couple you must decide how best to protect and guard your marriage in a way that maximizes the blessings of family and minimizes damage.

> Honor your father and mother, that everything may go well for you, and you may have a long life on earth. (Ephesians 6:2–3 GW)

> Hear, my son, your father's instruction, and forsake not your mother's teaching, for they are a graceful garland for your head and pendants for your neck. (Proverbs 1:8–9 ESV)

COUPLES ♥ CHALLENGE

♥ *Answer these questions and discuss with each other:*

> *Do I involve my family with intimate issues?*
>
> *Do I constantly have to ask my family for advice?*
>
> *Do I need my family's support (financial, emotional, physical presence) to survive?*
>
> *Do I side more with my family than my spouse?*

(If you answered yes often, you may want to consider that you may be too enmeshed.)

> *Do I have limited or no contact with my family?*
>
> *Do we never spend holidays with my family?*
>
> *Do I pride myself on not needing my family?*
>
> *Is there conflict that needs to be addressed?*

(If you answered yes often, you may be totally cut off. Consider whether you need to make some effort to connect or try to deal with conflict.)

EXPECTATIONS

> *What causes fights and quarrels among you? Don't they come from the desires that battle within you?*
>
> **James 4:1 NIV**

I (Carla) could author a book on this one—only because I have made all the mistakes you can make related to this topic. We all enter marriage with some expectations. Many are realistic and appropriate. We should expect our spouse to do certain things such as to be faithful and keep their vows, to stay, to treat us with respect, and to love and support us. There are several issues that expectations can bring about, though. Ask yourself these questions:

- Are my expectations realistic?

- Have I ever expressed these to my spouse?

- How do I manage unmet expectations?

The difficulty is that your expectations may seem reasonable and realistic to you, but are they? We must examine our expectations considering what marriage is designed to be. God does intend us to help meet some of the needs of our spouse—but he never intended another human being to meet the deepest needs of our hearts. Only God can fill that vacuum. Only God can consistently be everything we need. Marriage can be an incredible place of oneness and support, but our spouse will never meet all our expectations. So, we may need to realign them.

Does my spouse know what I expect? I am going to be bold and say this. Women, (I can say this since I am one) I think many times we play a game where we expect and want our spouse to know what we would like and need. So we don't tell them but then get mad when they don't know. Wives, may I again be bold and tell you: *they do not know!* We can continue to play that game and not get what we want, or we can be up-front and share our expectations. This doesn't guarantee that we will get what we would like, but it absolutely gives us a better shot.

How, then, do we respond when our expectations are unmet, even if they are realistic and requested? This is where the rubber meets the road. It is hard, because we feel disappointed, hurt, angry, or frustrated. But this is the place God will use to teach us deep and freeing truth. We will be disappointed in one another, we will feel let down, we will not get what we expected. This is a reality, but this is where God meets us. He can use every one of these unmet expectations to deepen our faith and trust in him, mature our character, and give us an opportunity to exhibit self-sacrificing love.

This doesn't mean that we cannot share our disappointment with our spouse, but that we openly and honestly share it, and then we must lay it down. If we don't, then a seed of bitterness and resentment can start to grow. It took me so long to learn this principle. I would tell Johnny something that I wanted or needed, but I would not lay it down. I would keep harping on it—reminding him, trying to change him and get him to be or do what I wanted. I was a broken record. It only served to frustrate me and drive him away. We want to allow God to teach us that he alone can fill every part of our heart. Then we can allow unfilled expectations to not derail us but take us deeper into the heart of our Father.

> As an example of suffering and patience, brothers, take the prophets who spoke in the name of the Lord. Behold, we consider those blessed who remain steadfast. (James 5:10 ESV)

> In all of this, you greatly rejoice, though now for a little while you may have had to suffer grief in all kinds of trials. (1 Peter 1:6 NIV)

COUPLES ♥ CHALLENGE

♥ *Do you have expectations that you have not shared with your spouse?*

♥ *Are you willing to share them? Be specific.*

♥ *When was the last time you expected something from your spouse that did not happen? What was your response?*

♥ *Can you see anything God may be wanting to teach you through this?*

WHEN LOVING HURTS

> *Greater love has no one than this, that someone lay down his life for his friends.*
>
> **John 15:13 ESV**

When we stood before each other on our wedding day and pledged to love and honor each other all the days of our lives, we did not imagine that love might hurt. I (Carla) really had no idea what I was saying "I do" to, let alone that it would ever hurt. I knew couples had disagreements, things they had to work through, but honestly did not see the rest of it coming! I did not understand what loving meant.

Loving hurts because when we choose to love, we choose to be vulnerable. Being vulnerable means we are open to being hurt. We have shared the deepest parts of ourselves with another human being; we are exposed. There are certainly varying levels of hurt. Some hurts are hard but not devastating, while others wound to our core.

When we are hurt by our spouse, it feels terrible. The emotions may be strong, heavy, even physically painful. Our emotions may scream loud and be overwhelming if we're not careful. To address this, we must do several things:

- Acknowledge the emotions and the hurt.

- Remember that emotions do not have intelligence.

- Remember that our emotions do not need to be in charge.

- Know that we can choose what to set our mind on.

In our marriages there will be times of hurt. We are sinful human beings, and we will say and do things that hurt each other. So, what do you do when you are hurt by your spouse? Here are two questions to ask yourself: Is it something that I can just overlook and let go? Is it something that must be addressed? The level of the offense and hurt will dictate what may need to happen for healing to occur. There may be times when we allow love to cover a multitude of sins. We may need to give greater grace to our spouse. We may need to examine our own heart to see if there is anything that we need to own. We may need to seek outside help.

Loving even when it hurts is part of marriage. It's knowing we will be hurt at times, seeing the ugliness, and still choosing by an act of our will to love, to forgive, and to work toward restoration. This is part of our covenant marriage story—love and redemption.

> Love does not insist on its own way; it is not irritable or resentful; it does not rejoice at wrong doings but rejoices with the truth. (1 Corinthians 13:4–8 ESV)

> Be kind to one another, tenderhearted, forgiving one another, as God in Christ forgave you. (Ephesians 4:32 ESV)

COUPLES ♥ CHALLENGE

♥ *Think about rating your hurt. The next time something offends or hurts you, use the following scale to rate the level of it.[2] It may be beneficial to your spouse for them to have an objective number to go with your description.*

> *1 = No big deal. I'm not even going to mention it.*
>
> *2 = We don't see it the same way; I may be wrong.*
>
> *3 = I don't agree, but I can live with it.*
>
> *4 = I disagree, but we will go with your way.*
>
> *5 = I don't agree and I can't be silent about this.*
>
> *6 = I don't approve, but I need more time to think about this.*
>
> *7 = I strongly disagree and I can't go along with this.*
>
> *8 = I am so upset I don't know what I am going to do.*
>
> *9 = No way! You go through with this and I quit.*
>
> *10 = Over my dead body!*

♥ *If the hurt or offense is a 5 or higher, you need to address it. Decide when, where, and how you need to do this. If hurts are deep and devasting, understand that you may need outside assistance (a coach or counselor) to work through the pain.*

---

2   Drs. Les & Leslie Parrott, *Saving Your Marriage Before It Starts* (Grand Rapids, MI: Zondervan, 2015), 149.

YOUR "SOLE" MATE

A wife is bound to her husband as long as he lives. But if her husband dies, she is free to marry anyone she wishes, but he must belong to the Lord.

I Corinthians 7:39 ESV

True confession: we like to watch Hallmark Christmas movies (concerning, I know). But there is nothing like watching the main character find their soul mate, finally kiss, and watch it begin to snow, which of course is the way all of them end. But unfortunately, that's not reality.

We have all heard about finding your soul mate. Well, I hate to say it, but the concept of each of us having one soul mate is not truth. It plays well in the movies, but nothing in God's Word teaches that concept. When you think about it, if there really was only one person for you, then when the first person messed up and married the wrong person, it would be a domino effect. Most everyone would then be with the wrong person.

One of the reasons that we need to debunk this is because if you believe there is only one person who is your soul mate, when you start to have problems and struggles in your marriage, the most logical conclusion is that you married the wrong person. In other words, this must not be your soul mate.

For believers who are following God's direction and will for their life, we certainly want to be wise in who we marry. We want to marry another believer who has a heart for God and a character that reflects this. Often, after we marry, we have moments when we think, *Oh no. This person is not who I thought they were.* The rose-colored glasses come off, and we realize how different we are from each other; we see things we might not have seen at the beginning. We may even ask; *Did I marry the wrong person?*

The answer is likely NO! Depending on your situation, you may need to seek counseling, but God grants us the chance to become the sole (one and only) mate to our spouse. So, what does that look like? It has several aspects:

- I choose to cherish the spouse I have.

- I choose not to compare them to anyone else.

- I focus on what they are, not on what they are not.

- I set my mind on what is good, lovely, and admirable in my spouse (see Philippians 4:8).

- I choose to be content with what I have.

- I learn to love and serve them out of reverence for God.

We repeat this process over and over. It allows our mindset to change, and when our mindset changes, so does our behavior, and then ultimately our feelings start to change. This order must be right. We align our minds, which shapes our behavior, which leads to a renewal of our emotions. The amazing, beautiful thing is that God can do this. We can have new eyes to see our spouse. We can find joy and delight in them. We can become the sole mate of our spouse.

> House and wealth are inherited from the fathers, but a prudent wife is from the LORD. (Proverbs 19:14 ESV)

> Above all, keep loving one another earnestly, since love covers a multitude of sins. (1 Peter 4:8 ESV)

COUPLES ♥ CHALLENGE

♥ *How can I make my spouse feel loved, honored, and supported today?*

♥ *Do whatever you just thought about.*

♥ *If you are not certain, ask your spouse how they would like to be loved, honored, or supported. See the 5 Questions from Week 16.*

♥ *Verbalize one thing you appreciate about your spouse.*

♥ *Later in the week, repeat this process.*

HEAD, NOT HEART

> *Male and female he created them.*
>
> **Genesis 1:27 NLT**

Picture this: A wife comes home after a stressful day, and she can't wait to see her husband so she can talk through everything with him. He gets home, they sit on the couch, and she begins going through what's on her mind. Several times in the conversation, he interrupts her with his "fix" for her problem. She finally has enough and, frustrated, says, "I don't want you to fix anything. I just want you to listen. If you loved me, you would understand that."

Picture this: A husband comes home after a stressful day. He can't wait to go out to his workshop, unwind, and think over the day's issues. His wife hears him come in and greets him with a kiss and asks him, "How was your day?" He responds, "Fine." Her intuition tells her that he's more stressed than usual and presses him, "Are you sure everything's okay?" He responds, "Yes, I'm fine." And heads out to his workshop. His wife feels shut out. She thinks to herself, *I know something is bothering him. If he loves me, why won't he talk to me?*

Sound familiar? I could give you dozens of stories from my own marriage about the diverse ways men and women handle things. The key is this: do not let brain differences become heart issues. Dr. J. Budziszewski, a professor of philosophy at the University of Texas, was teaching a class when a student challenged him by asking, "Aren't men and women just the same except for their anatomy? It is just society that makes distinctions." The professor answered her, "As different as men and women are physically, the most profound difference between them is the way their brains work."[3]

Modern research tells us that. In general, men's and women's brains operate differently. One is not better than the other; they're just different. It's this difference, along with other temperament and personality differences, that leads to much of the challenges men and women face in their relationships with each other. When their spouse doesn't react the way they want, they make it a heart issue by thinking, *They must not love me!* The reality is their response has nothing to do with them loving the other person. They are simply wired differently.

While I know this can be frustrating and we think the way we see things is correct, God has not designed us this way. Just because our spouse doesn't think like we do doesn't mean they're defective. Psalm 139 tells us that we are "fearfully and wonderfully made" by God (v. 14 ESV). We need to celebrate the distinctive ways that God made us different from each other.

---

3   https://garythomas.com/2020/06/24/delicious-difference/

Embrace the differences in your spouse and focus on how you can complement each other and create a better "one" than you could ever be separately.

God's design is perfect. He made no mistakes when he made you and your spouse. But as in everything else in this world, we are impacted by the fall and sin. Our thinking is not always righteous and in line with God's heart and desires. However, it is not our job to transform our spouse. That is something only God can do. He will often use us in that process as "iron sharpening iron" (see Proverbs 27:17). Our focus needs to be on loving our spouse for who God created them to be, not on what they are not in our eyes, and allowing him to transform us into the very best version of ourselves.

> For you formed my inward parts; you knitted me together in my mother's womb. I praise you, for I am fearfully and wonderfully made. Wonderful are your works. (Psalm 139:13–14 ESV)

COUPLES ♥ CHALLENGE

♥ *Each of you take a piece of paper and make a list. What are some of the key differences you have seen in the way your spouse thinks, responds, or acts differently than you when in similar situations? When done, compare your lists.*

♥ *Go through your lists and categorize each difference you wrote down as being a **1)** gender difference, **2)** personality/ temperament difference, or **3)** family of origin difference.*

♥ *Looking at the lists together, how can you leverage those differences so they enhance your marriage rather than being a source of conflict or irritation?*

♥ *Look up the online video "It's Not About the Nail" (Jason Headley). Watch and discuss it together. Have you seen a similar situation in your marriage? What did you learn from it?*

LEAN INTO YOUR STRENGTHS

> *But each of you has your own gift from God; one has this gift, another has that.*
>
> **I Corinthians I:7 NIV**

Many experts in the field of psychology tell us we are drawn to strengths we see in others, especially if it is the opposite of our perceived weakness. Hence, the opposites-attract theory. Whether or not this is always true, it is certainly a reality that many people marry someone who has strengths that are opposite their own. Think about when you first started dating your spouse. What drew you to them? What were you fascinated or enamored by? It was likely a strength that is part of their God-given DNA.

Our story is certainly that of opposites attracting. Johnny was quiet, highly intelligent, somewhat like a renaissance man, spontaneous, and adventuresome. He was interested in so many different things, and he was gifted in multiple ways. I found this very attractive because he was so opposite of me. I talk more, see the world as black and white, color between the lines, am extremely focused, and am disciplined to a fault. There is not a spontaneous bone in my body; I like to schedule my spontaneity.

Can you imagine the fireworks we've experienced? (No, not in a good way). What I found interesting and attractive while dating became total frustration for me in marriage. So, what did I do? I focused on everything Johnny didn't do, on his weaknesses, and on how we could shore them up. In essence, I wanted to rewire him! I felt my plan gave him much more potential than leaving him to his own devices, and I spent years trying to change his weaknesses. Because my focus was on his weaknesses (or my perception of them), I disregarded what his strengths were. I missed enjoying, celebrating, and benefiting from his strengths.

Think about a weakness that one of you may have. Let's take organization for example. If you're not organized, then it's not one of your strengths. Even if you spent all your time trying to improve that weakness, how much improvement do you think you will get? Will organization become a top strength? Probably not. We can spend untoward time and energy for minimal change. I'm not saying we can't and shouldn't work on areas that we may need to improve, but I am offering the challenge to think about spending more time strengthening the gifts you have.

In your marriage, especially if you have extremely different temperaments, it can be so tempting to put all the focus on each other's weaknesses. As believers we always want to allow the Holy Spirit to change us into the image of Jesus. But in our marriage we need to magnify the strengths in our spouse and marginalize the weaknesses. What can be metamorphic is when we focus on the strengths in each other, we often find they balance our weakness. We find beauty in what God blends together.

> There are different kinds of gifts, but the same Spirit distributes them. There are different kinds of service, but the same Lord. (1 Corinthians 12:4–5 NIV)

> I have filled him with the Spirit of God, with wisdom, understanding, with knowledge and with all kinds of skills. (Exodus 31:3 NIV)

COUPLES ♥ CHALLENGE

♥ *Each of you tell your spouse one strength they have that you really admire.*

♥ *Share one weakness that you know you have.*

♥ *Does your spouse agree with you?*

♥ *Can you see where any of your weaknesses are balanced by a strength in your spouse?*

HOW DO YOU WANT TO BE LOVED?

> *Let no debt remain outstanding except the continuing debt to love one another, for whoever loves others has fulfilled the law.*
>
> **Romans 13:8 NIV**

Loaded question, right? Do you know the answer for yourself and your spouse? If not, you need to find out.

We all need love, but we all want and need it in different ways. I'm referring to our love languages. There are assessments we can take to help determine how we want to be loved, and many couples do this as part of their premarital preparation. Even if you did take one of these assessments, I would encourage you to do it again. We have found that many couples change their love languages over the years.

Why does this matter? Because if you are trying to love your spouse either in the way you think they want to be loved, or in the way you like to be loved, you might be totally missing the mark.

For years, Johnny did for me what his love language was, and I did for him what mine was. We were trying to love each other from the perspective of how we wanted to be loved. My love language was acts of service. I wanted the grass mowed, the car maintained, the needed repairs around the house noticed and done. Johnny's love language was gifts. So guess what? I got lots of gifts. I'm not knocking the gift; I love a great purse as well as the next girl, but the grass was high and needed to be mowed. I, on the other hand, did acts of service for Johnny, which was my love language, but I did not always give the best gifts.

For someone who has the love language of gifts, missing a birthday or special event without an "expression" of a gift is a huge deal. If you don't have that language, then it may seem crazy or ridiculous, but it screams to them that you don't care and you don't know them. There can be deep hurt when we attempt to love our spouse without knowing their language. Couples may be "trying" to love their spouse, but because it is not the way their spouse receives love, it can cause a drift in the marriage, which creates distance because one spouse feels unloved. The intent may be right, but the method may be wrong.

Understanding the love language of our spouse is one way to learn to be intentional in the way we love. We can learn to love them in a way that resonates with them. This can be so impactful because it meets their need for love. We may not totally get it or understand why they respond that way, but it's not about us. It's about them. When we choose to know and intentionally love our spouse in the language that is meaningful to them, we are acting out agape love.

> Do nothing out of selfish ambition or vain conceit. Rather, in humility, value others above yourself. (Philippians 2:3 NIV)

> A new command I give you: Love one another. As I have loved you, so you must love one another. (John 13:34 NIV)

COUPLES ♥ CHALLENGE

♥ Do an online assessment on love languages. (We recommend the 5 Love Languages at www.5lovelanguages.com or the 7 Love Styles Test at www.truity.com.)

♥ Share the results with each other. You probably have a primary and a secondary language.

♥ Based on your language(s), make certain you explain the dialect (e.g., "quality time" may mean totally different things to the two of you).

♥ Tell your spouse one way you would like to be "loved" this upcoming week.

C.H.A.S.E. (PAY ATTENTION, HUSBANDS!)

> *Cherish her, and she will exalt you; if you embrace her, she will honor you.*
>
> **Proverbs 4:8 CSB**

In the Mel Gibson movie *What Women Want*, Gibson's character has an accident that allows him to hear what women are thinking. He now knows what they want. Of course, ultimately this ends up causing him trouble. But, husbands, wouldn't it be awesome if you knew exactly what your wife wanted?

Now, what do women want in their relationships? C.H.A.S.E. is our acronym for what a woman wants. While we realize that this will not be true for all women, we believe it covers many of their core desires.

C = Cherished

If you ask a woman what it means to be cherished, she will use terms like *honored, special, significant, valued,* and *treasured.* Most men don't understand the word ☺. God created us to be relational, and he brought Eve to Adam to be in "relationship" with him. Women have a deep desire to be seen, heard, and wanted.

H=Honesty

Relationships are built on honesty. The foundation of marriage is based on trust in that honesty. We need to know that our spouse is open with us and not holding back, being real, and allowing us to see the true person. Husbands, this means not withholding information, even in a misguided attempt to protect your wife. Tell her the truth in love (see Ephesians 4:15).

A=Affection/Attention

Yes, this means sex, but it also means much more. It is the tender way you touch her that says, "You are mine; you belong to me." It is the look or the words that are spoken that convey your desire for her. Affection is what keeps the flame alive. It is the continual pursuit of your wife that says, "I choose you over and over."

S=Security

Security means different things to different women. The root, though, is the concept that you, as her husband, are willing and able to do whatever it takes to make her feel secure and safe. This may mean financial provision or willingness to do whatever is needed for the benefit of your home and family. It may mean a protective posture that promises you will keep the family safe from what might destroy or damage them. Security means you have her back, forever and always.

E= Eyes Only

(I [Carla] love this one.) As the husband, you have eyes only for your wife. You must choose to have her be your definition of beauty. You see her as the one that delights you. You honor her above all others. You make the daily choice to treat her as if she is Eve (meaning the only one for you). On the day you got married, you, in essence, said to your wife, "I choose you above all others, those I have met and anyone I will ever meet."

If a husband will C.H.A.S.E. his wife like this, I can promise you it will be a beautiful catch.

> For no one ever hated his own flesh, but nourishes and cherishes it. (Ephesians 5:29 ESV)

> Do not lie to each other, seeing that you have taken off your old self with its practices. (Colossians 3:9 ESV)

> Husbands, love your wives, just as Christ loved the church and gave himself up for her. (Ephesians 5:25 NIV)

COUPLES ♥ CHALLENGE

♥ *Wives, do you agree with this acronym describing what women truly want? If not, tell your husband what you desire.*

♥ *Husbands, what part of this is hard for you?*

♥ *Wives, what does affection mean to you? Tell your husband how you want to be touched, spoken to, etc.*

♥ *Wives, security can mean different things. Tell your husband one thing that he does that makes you feel secure.*

♥ *Wives, share one thing that would make you feel like your husband has eyes for you only.*

C.A.S.H. (LISTEN UP, WIVES!)

> *So again, I say, each man must love his wife as he loves himself, and the wife must respect her husband.*
>
> **Ephesians 5:33 NLT**

What do husbands want in a marriage? I know you may think, *ask one hundred men and you will get one hundred answers,* but both Christian and secular research comes up with a similar set of desires expressed by most men.

We talk in terms of desires and not needs, as some often talk about. Our acronym for what most men say they want is C.A.S.H. (I know you may be surprised it's not S.E.X.) The deepest needs we each have can only be met by God; no person can ever satisfy those needs. If your spouse's desires are consistent with biblical principles, you should strive to meet those needs.

C=Companionship

While women generally build a relationship by talking, men build a relationship by doing things together. A man's idea of spending quality time with his wife usually involves doing some activity together. Learn to enjoy (or at least tolerate) the things your husband enjoys. If he likes golf and you don't, try driving the cart while he plays. Maybe he is a football fan. If you don't know the difference between a quarterback and a cornerback, take some time and learn. Better yet, take the initiative and find activities you both enjoy. It will be worth the effort.

A=Admiration/Affirmation

For many men, one of their greatest fears is failure, especially at not being a good husband, provider, or father, or in their career. Even though he may never say it, that fear of failure often drives a man, and it may explain why men crave respect from their wives, children, and peers. Your husband needs to know that you believe in him. We always teach that a wife needs to be her husband's biggest cheerleader in public. If you need to correct him, make sure you do so in private, just the two of you.

S=Sexual Fulfillment

No surprise here, but this is number one for most men. What may surprise you is that this desire seems to be rooted in their need to be desired by their wife. Men want to be wanted. God created us so the act of sex would bind us to each other physically, emotionally, and spiritually. Sometimes we may be tempted to use sex as a weapon by denying our spouse, and that is a dangerous game to play. Paul warns us in his letter to the Corinthians not to withhold sexual intimacy from each other except by mutual agreement (see 1 Corinthians 7:5). Sexual intimacy is one of the great gifts God has given to married couples. Treat it with the reverence and respect it deserves.

H=Home as a Refuge

More than ever, men (and women) need their home to be a safe haven against the culture in which they live. While a man's self-esteem is often grounded in his career, as the world grows more hostile toward Christianity, the home becomes a place to find safety, support, and encouragement. This quote from Marvin J. Ashton sums it up: "Home should be an anchor, a port in a storm, a refuge, a happy place in which to dwell, a place where we are loved and where we can love."[4]

Two people are better off than one, for they can help each other succeed. If one person falls, the other can reach out and help. But someone who falls alone is in real trouble. (Ecclesiastes 4:9–10 NLT)

---

4   https://www.deseret.com/1992/10/10/20764901/home-should-be-the-place-to-find-renewed-strength

COUPLES ♥ CHALLENGE

♥ *Husbands, do you agree with the desires we listed as the desires most men have? Why or why not?*

♥ *Husbands, what needs would you add?*

♥ *Husbands, make a list of your most important needs. Share them with your spouse and explain what you mean for each need.*

♥ *Wives, what are some specific ways for you to meet the needs of your husband?*

WEEK 28

KEEP THE FIRES BURNING

> *You have captured my heart, my treasure, my bride. You hold it hostage with one glance of your eyes, with a single jewel of your necklace. Your love delights me, my treasure, my bride. Your love is better than wine, your perfume more fragrant than spices. Your lips are as sweet as nectar, my bride. Honey and milk are under your tongue.*
>
> **Song of Solomon 4:9–11 NLT**

What do you do with the Song of Solomon? Is it an allegory about God's love for Israel? Is it just poetry? It doesn't mention God or have any theological discourse, so why is it part of the Old Testament? Churches have even told members, "Don't read it until you are married." '

I believe the book is God's blessing on passionate love, romance, and sex in the marriage relationship. Rabbi Adam Greenwald put it this way: "If you've never read the Song of Songs in bed with someone that you love ... you are missing out on one of the great religious experiences that our tradition has to offer! The Song of Songs (Shir ha-Shirim in Hebrew) is an unabashedly sensuous, even at times quite erotic, paean to love."[5]

When we teach about love, we often emphasize that *agape*, the word the Bible uses for unconditional love, is not an emotion. It is a verb that focuses on how you act toward each other, not how you feel. I can choose to love you even if I don't like you or the way you are acting.

So, are feelings of romance and passion wrong or something not to be desired in marriage? Of course not! You can't build a marriage on romance, but it sure makes it more fun. The Song of Solomon emphasizes that having passion and romance in your marriage is a good thing and to be sought after. Now, how do you keep that fire of passion and romance burning amid the day-to-day challenges of marriage?

Have you ever been to a restaurant and seen a couple sitting across from each other eating their meal, and yet they never engage with each other? As you watch them, you think, *They must be married.* Why do we think that way? Because all too often that seems to be true. The spark, the engagement, the excitement of being with the one you love, seems to be gone. But it doesn't have to be that way. You must stoke the fire.

How do you do that? As we looked at in the devotional on C.H.A.S.E., keep the pursuit going even after you are married.

---

5   https://www.myjewishlearning.com/article/song-of-songs

Take a clue from how you pursued each other before you were married. Date nights, love notes, unexpected gifts, flowers for no reason at all other than to say "I love you." It's not a hard thing to do. You must be intentional about keeping your marriage the priority as you navigate children, careers, family, church, and all the other things that happen in life. As the company Nike proclaims, "Just do it!"

> I am my lover's. I'm all he wants. I'm all the world to him! (Song of Solomon 7:10 MSG)

> Place me like a seal over your heart, like a seal on your arm. For love is as strong as death, its jealousy as enduring as the grave. Love flashes like fire, the brightest kind of flame. Many waters cannot quench love, nor can rivers drown it. (Song of Solomon 8:6–7 NLT)

COUPLES ♥ CHALLENGE

♥ *Make date nights a priority. Put them on the calendar and protect them.*

♥ *Surprise your spouse this week with something you know they enjoy.*

♥ *Make a date jar. Each of you writes on a slip of paper date-night ideas you would like to do and put them into the jar. Once a week, pull a slip out and do it.*

♥ *Check out* **The Adventure Challenge for Couples.**
(www.theadventurechallenge.com)

DO YOU SPEAK THE SAME LANGUAGE?

Come, let's go down and confuse the people with different languages. Then they won't be able to understand each other.

Genesis 11:7 NLT

Communication is a topic of utmost importance. Most of us do not enter marriage knowing how to communicate. We quickly wonder if we even speak the same language. It may seem like when God desired to spread all the people over the whole earth (Genesis 11). He confused their language and they scattered, and we may feel that same confusion between us and our spouse. If by chance we speak the same language, there are probably different dialects.

The ability to express ourselves via words, inflections, gestures, and body language with clarity is an acquired skill for most of us. Since we know what we want to convey, we assume that it's crystal clear to our spouse. The problem is that our spouse is filtering what we're saying through both their visual lens and their ear buds—and their ear buds may be on a totally different frequency. What we are certain we said, may not be what their ears heard. If by some miracle, the actual words were heard, their brain then processes those words through their stored memory, experiences, and emotions. Therefore, what we thought we said may not be what they heard.

So, how in the world do we learn to communicate so our spouse receives an accurate message? There are several key components:

- Choose your words carefully. They matter!

- Make certain your verbal and nonverbal match.

- State what you want or need in a clear manner. (Don't assume they know.)

- Use "I" messages (I think … , I feel …).

God's Word has much to say about the power of our words. Words can wound or heal—and they reveal what is in our heart. Spoken words cannot be unspoken.

I often think of the visual we did with our children one time to illustrate this point. We gave them each a tube of toothpaste and told them to squeeze it out as fast as they could. Then we told them to put the toothpaste back in the tube. Of course, that's impossible, but it was fun to watch them try and have the toothpaste all over everything. We all know the point. We can't put back what has been said. I so wish I had heeded this principle earlier in our married life. I said things I could not take back; I wounded using my tongue.

When communicating with your spouse, decide how significant the issue is. If it is important, then make certain you have the appropriate time, space, and setting to discuss it. Removing barriers to help with important conversations is critical. If your spouse is tired, hungry, sick, pressed for time, or upset, then it may not be the best time to have the discussion. If you need to schedule it, then schedule it. Effective communication is one of the keys to a satisfying relationship. Couples who are willing to develop this skill can enhance their relationship on multiple levels and avoid unnecessary confusion and heartache.

Evil words destroy; Godly skill rebuilds. (Proverbs 11:9 NLT)

A gentle answer quiets anger, but a harsh one stirs it up. (Proverbs 15:1 NIV)

COUPLES ♥ CHALLENGE

♥ *Take turns answering these questions using a scale of 1–10, where 1 = poorly and 10 = exceptional:*

How well do you think you communicate?

How well do you think your spouse communicates?

Do you agree? Were you shocked by the other's answer? How do you reconcile the difference in scores if there is one?

What do you think is your strongest area of communication as a couple?

FAILURE TO COMMUNICATE

> *Let every person be quick to listen, slow to speak,*
> *and slow to become angry.*
>
> **James 1:19 ESV**

In the last devotional, we discussed how critical effective communication is to a satisfying relationship. Communication is the sum of verbal and nonverbal sharing of yourself with your spouse, so anything that impacts either or both of these will cause a barrier. Let's examine a few things that impact sharing.

♥ **Gender differences**

Men and women speak and process language differently. In general, women talk to develop rapport, while men talk to report. Women may talk to process a problem, while men may want to think about the problem before they talk about it. Men may want to fix a problem when they hear it, while a woman may just want to share it.

This area was huge for Johnny and me. It was a game-changer when I learned to say to him, "I just need for you to listen. I don't want you to fix it."

♥ Different dictionary

Words can have different meanings. We may be using the same word but have totally different meanings for it. We can't assume our words mean the same thing to another person. I think "a few minutes" means about fifteen; Johnny thinks it means two or three. We're still working through this, but you can see that our words do not mean the same thing.

♥ Nonverbal communication

Expressions on our face, our body position, the tension in our body, and our hand movements or gestures all speak loudly. If the verbal (what we're saying) does not match the nonverbal, the nonverbal wins. You can see this when your spouse says they are "fine" but their body language says otherwise.

♥ Defensiveness

Sometimes we miss the totality of the message because we immediately become defensive and are thinking about our rebuttal. We think we know exactly what they are going to say, so we assume the conclusion. By doing this, we miss the opportunity to hear what our spouse really wants to convey.

♥ Negative/judgmental mindset

A negative mindset means we are filtering everything that
is communicated through the negative; that is all we hear.
The negative is a filter that may have developed based on
past hurts, disappointments, or anger, and it will damage
or destroy any ability to have meaningful communication.
This mindset must be acknowledged, removed, and
replaced with a new filter to move toward healing.

Some of these barriers may just need to be recognized and
respected as part of our unique differences. Other barriers are
deeply rooted in past hurts and patterns of behaviors that may
require the assistance of a professional counselor or marriage
coach. Either way, removing a barrier requires a willingness to
do work. This work may seem too hard at times, but in the end
we can move toward increased intimacy in our marriage.

A person's wisdom yields patience; it is to one's glory to
overlook an offense. (Proverbs 19:11 ESV)

The way of a fool is right in his own eyes, but a wise man listens
to advise. (Proverbs 12:15 ESV)

COUPLES ♥ CHALLENGE

♥ *What is one communication barrier you want to work on?*

♥ *Is there anything you do not feel "safe" talking about?*

♥ *What is one small change you can make to avoid or remove a barrier?*

♥ *What percentage of the time do you think your verbal and nonverbal match?*

HOW GOOD IS YOUR HEARING?

Understand this, my dear brothers and sisters:
You must all be quick to listen, slow to speak,
and slow to get angry.

James 1:19 NLT

Isn't it interesting that this verse lists hearing first, as the positive directive? Ask yourself, *How often am I quick to listen instead of planning what I am going to say?*

Communication is not just the ability to express ourselves, but also to listen to what the other person is saying. Listening—truly hearing someone—is a rare and precious gift. It has always been so, but it is more valuable today because of the constant bombardment from every imaginable source vying for our attention.

So, why should we learn to listen well?

- It gives us an opportunity to understand our spouse.

- We can learn something from them.

- We can enjoy them.

- It conveys value and interest.

Why is listening so hard?

- It takes time.

- It takes intentionality.

- It takes being unselfish.

- It takes loving someone else enough to care about what is in their heart.

How can you show that we are listening?

- Don't multitask (i.e., put the phone, watch, tablet away).

- Look the person in the eye.

- Ask clarifying questions or questions that show interest.

- Don't fidget and don't leave the room.

- Lean forward with an open arm position.

What are some barriers to listening well?

- Mental overload

- Short attention span

- Selective attention (hearing what we want to)

- Impatience with our spouse's talking speed

How can we overcome the barriers?

- Identify which barriers are present.

- Determine the best place and time to have important conversations.

- Establish boundaries for these conversation—location, time, no distracting items, topic.

- Figure out where there are any things that can be changed, adjusted, or removed that would make listening easier.

Learning to listen well is a gift to our spouse. It has also been an area that Johnny and I have struggled and grown in. For Johnny to really listen to me, and indicate in all the ways just listed that he is hearing me, is one of the best things he can do for me. I feel heard, seen, valued, and cherished when he does this.

The pinnacle of listening is moving toward empathic listening, or approaching every conversation with the intent to understand our spouse. It allows us to have a more accurate interpretation of what they have said. We can move beyond just the words and actually hear the intent of the message. It can give us greater clarity to also "hear" what our spouse may not be saying. By asking questions, we can send a strong message that we want to know more. We want to understand.

Being willing to learn to listen well is, many times, a giant step in healing past wounds and offenses. Listening is a powerful tool to begin to understand our spouse, and listening well is the doorway to loving well.

> To respond to a matter before you hear about it shows foolishness and brings shame. (Proverbs 18:13 VOICE)

Let the wise hear and increase in learning, and the one who understands obtain guidance. (Proverbs 1:5 ESV)

COUPLES ♥ CHALLENGE

♥ *Share a barrier you have when it comes to listening well (there may be ones other than those listed above).*

♥ *What is one tangible thing you can do to improve your listening skills?*

♥ *Ask each other these questions. On a scale of 1–10, with 1 = terrible and 10 = terrific ...*

> *How do you rate yourself as a listener?*
>
> *How do you rate your spouse as a listener?*
>
> *Are you close with your numbers? Did it surprise you?*

♥ *Decide on one area where you would like to see improvement. Set one goal, make it specific, and set a date to review it.*

A MATTER OF PERSPECTIVE

What do you see?

This Photo by Unknown Author is licensed under CC BY-ND.

For my thoughts are not your thoughts, neither are your ways my ways, declares the LORD. For as the heavens are higher than the earth, so are my ways higher than your ways and my thoughts than your thoughts.

Isaiah 55:8–9 ESV

We have all seen images like this. Some of us immediately see a rabbit while some see a duck. Once we know that it can be both, most folks can turn their head, squint their eyes, and maybe get their brain to see the other image. Sometimes, though, no matter what we do, we just don't see the second image.

Perspective is like that. We see so clearly from our own point of view. We see it, think it, and feel it, so it must be true. This is our reality. The problem is that our spouse is possibly looking through a different-colored lens. They also see it, think it, and feel it, so it must be true. That is their reality. Now we have "opposite" things that we both feel and know to be true!

Understanding perspective in marriage is critical to learning to forge a deeper connection without damaging each other. Different perspectives do not have to mean one is right and one is wrong. It may just mean we see it differently. If we allow it, different perspectives can mean a chance to grow and stretch. They give us a chance to try to see something in a new way. For me (Carla), this has been a hard place. So many times, my perspective on something was different from Johnny's, and I had such a difficult time learning that my perspective was not always right—or, even if it was right, that his was not wrong.

In our marriage, this came up with the issue of money. I struggled with the fact that, for me, money represented security. My perspective was that we save, plan, and budget so we have what you need. Johnny viewed money as something to be used for others and experiences. Neither one of us was wrong, but our different perspectives led to numerous conflicts over money. We need to allow each other to share their perspective and be willing to ask questions, clarify, and challenge so we avoid misperceptions. We may still have different perspectives, but we want to be clear.

As believers, none of us have total truth or clarity on all issues. As we grow in Christ, we change. God renews our minds and aligns our hearts, and our behavior ultimately reflects these changes. We will likely change our perspectives on different things over our lifetime. In a marriage of two believers, we can allow different perspectives to challenge us and give us the opportunity to glean new insights from each other. We can be willing to change our mind, see another possibility, and be tender with each other all along the way.

> There is a way that seems right to a man, but its end is the way to death. (Proverbs 14:12 ESV)

> As obedient children do not be conformed to the passions of your former ignorance, but as he who called you is holy, you also be holy in all your conduct. (1 Peter 1:14–15 ESV)

COUPLES ♥ CHALLENGE

♥ *When was the last time you and your spouse had a difference in perspective?*

♥ *Have you each had a chance to explain your perspective? If not, do it now.*

♥ *Can you see anything differently now?*

♥ *Try to put yourself in your spouse's shoes. How does that look and feel?*

♥ *What are topics or areas you consistently view through different lenses?*

FORGE AHEAD WITH CONFLICT

> *Get rid of all bitterness, rage, anger, harsh words,*
> *and slander, as well as all types of evil behavior.*
> *Instead, be kind to each other, tenderhearted,*
> *forgiving one another, just as God through*
> *Christ has forgiven you.*
>
> **Ephesians 4:31–32 NLT**

Carla and I have had our share of conflicts over the years. Some were minor, others were not so minor. We have both said things we regret. Things have never gotten physical, though she has threatened to cut off various parts of me. It has at times been loud. And I am sad to say, it has not always been healthy.

Great marriages aren't characterized by a lack of conflict but by the way the spouses face the conflict that inevitably comes. If we are in a relationship, conflict will occur. It is even more likely in relationships where we do most of our life together, such as marriage and family. The key is learning to handle conflict in a healthy way.

So, how should we look at conflict? Let's start with a goal: The goal, when we are faced with a conflict, is to resolve the conflict in a way that recognizes the needs and desires of both the husband and wife while preserving and enhancing the unity and health of the marriage.

The tagline for our ministry is "Forging a marriage that flourishes in all seasons." That image of forging—heating and applying pressure to the metal to conform it to the shape desired—is a picture of what God does in marriage. Conflict is the forge that creates strong, vibrant marriages. God using conflict to mold us into the image of Christ is a reason to celebrate conflict when it comes our way!

So, what can conflict do for our marriage?

- Every conflict we resolve is confirmation that our marriage is strong. Marriages that don't learn to handle conflict in a healthy way often don't survive.

- Conflict keeps us real, causes us to confront ourselves, sheds light on something we may not have seen, and clears the air. The conflicts we face in marriage become a key aspect of the Holy Spirit's process of sanctification. Conflict is where we see the principle of "iron sharpening iron" in action.

- Our love and marriage are ordained by God, and learning to handle conflict and still love each other despite our flaws is one of the most important things we can ever do. It becomes a reflection of God's love for his children despite our many flaws.

- We learn to give our spouse the same grace God has given each of us. Like in the parable of the servant who is forgiven his debt (Matthew 18:21–35), we can extend grace, mercy, and forgiveness to our spouse.

- Our marriages can become the haven that enables us to face the other challenges of life together. As we look back at the conflicts and challenges we have overcome, they can become the ebenezer (1 Samuel 7) or stones of remembrance for our marriage (1 Samuel 7:12). We know we can thrive as a couple amid conflict because we have done so before.

Don't use foul or abusive language. Let everything you say be good and helpful, so that your words will be an encouragement to those who hear them. (Ephesians 4:29 NLT)

Make allowance for each other's faults and forgive anyone who offends you. Remember, the Lord forgave you, so you must forgive others. (Colossians 3:13 NLT)

COUPLES ♥ CHALLENGE

♥ *Take a few minutes to recount the conflicts you have faced in the past. How did God use those conflicts to shape you individually and as a couple?*

♥ *What are some specific areas in your marriage right now where God might be using conflict to refine you and your marriage?*

♥ *How might a change in attitude about conflict change the way you approach it?*

T.R.A.S.H. – TIMING IS EVERYTHING

> *Don't sin by letting anger control you. Think about it overnight and remain silent.*
>
> **Psalm 4:4 NLT**

I n boxing, before the match begins, the referee brings both fighters to the center of the ring and goes over the rules. No biting, no gouging, no punches below the belt, and other rules for the match. With that taken care of, the boxers go to their corners and the bout begins.

Now, you and your spouse don't have referees for your conflicts, but you should have some rules of engagement. Paul tells us to glorify God in everything we do (1 Corinthians 10:31), including how we deal with conflict in our relationships. Conflict can help you forge a stronger marriage if you do it the right way, so we encourage you to come up with guidelines for how you will deal with conflict.

One of the key things you want to consider is the right time to deal with the conflicts that arise in your marriage. Psalm 4:4 tells us to not sin in our anger and to instead sleep on it so we can have a clear mind. Paul tells us that we have a sound mind and self-discipline in all that we do.

As counselors, we use the acronym T.R.A.S.H. to help couples know when the time may not be right to manage the conflict. To manage it well, you want to be at your best whenever possible.

T is for tired.

Why does it seem that conflict tends to occur after you've had a long day and are exhausted? Sometimes it's the fatigue itself that creates an opportunity for conflict. If one of you is too tired to think rationally, then acknowledge the issue, put it off until a better time, and go to bed. Schedule a time when you're rested and thinking clearly to tackle the issue.

R is for rushed.

You may be getting ready for work in the morning or heading to your son's ball game. This is not the ideal time to deal with conflicts. Your anxiety levels have already risen, and you can't give the issue the time it deserves. Trying to deal with issues when one or both of you are rushed is unwise. The best course of action is to acknowledge what is going on and agree to discuss it later.

A is for angry.

Whether you were already upset about something or the conflict at hand has pushed you to anger, call a timeout.

Anger is driven by emotions, and emotions are not rational. Dealing with conflict while angry often causes deep wounds that must be addressed before you can address the original conflict. We often say and do things we regret when we try to resolve the conflict while we are emotionally compromised. Take a thirty-minute break, go walk the dog, watch TV, or do something else that will allow your emotions to cool. Then you can resume dealing with the conflict in a rational way.

S is for sick.

You want both of you to be at your best emotionally and physically. I once heard a story about a husband who told his wife he wanted a divorce while she was in the hospital. Can you believe it? Whether the illness is a headache, a case of the flu, or any other situation where one of you is physically compromised, choose the wise course of putting off and attempting to resolve the conflict until you are both in better health.

H is for hungry.

I know this sounds crazy, but some people don't think well when they're hungry. That said, there's an easy remedy. Get something to eat and deal with the conflict in a healthy way.

In any of these situations, don't fake your condition. Don't use any of these to avoid dealing with conflict. In all these situations, acknowledge the conflict, schedule a time to talk after the impediment has been taken care of, and agree to resolve the issue or issues when you both are at your best. That's what love does.

For God did not give us a spirit of timidity or cowardice or fear, but [He has given us a spirit] of power and of love and of sound judgment and personal discipline [abilities that result in a calm, well-balanced mind and self-control]. (2 Timothy 1:7 AMP)

COUPLES ♥ CHALLENGE

♥ Think back on some of the conflicts and arguments you have experienced in your marriage. Did you ever violate the principles of T.R.A.S.H.? What were the results when you did?

♥ What are your "rules of engagement"? Discuss and come up with guidelines you agree on for how you are going to deal with conflict. Here are some ideas to get you going:

> Pray together before dealing with the conflict.
>
> T.R.A.S.H.
>
> No arguing in front of children.
>
> No arguing in public.
>
> Keep it conversational.
>
> Take a timeout when you're emotionally heated.

CONFLICT – MONEY MATTERS

> *So, in everything, do to others what you would*
> *have them do to you, for this sums up the*
> *Law and the Prophets.*
>
> **Matthew 7:12 NIV**

As we talked about in the last devotional reading, conflict can be a vehicle used to forge ahead in your marriage. You better believe that there will be plenty of opportunities that come in all sizes and shapes. Marriage inevitably reveals things in us and our spouse that can cause conflict. Over the next couple of weeks we are going to examine some common areas of conflict.

We will start with finances since this is one of the top issues for many couples. Finances represent not just how much money you make, spend, or save, but also what it means to you. As we mentioned earlier, this was one of our biggest struggles.

Johnny and I looked at money differently, so money represented different things to each of us. It may mean security, freedom, opportunities, influence, meeting your needs, significance, or generosity to others.

If money represents security to you, but your spouse considers it a source of blessing to others, this can cause conflict. Neither position is right or wrong, but money is tied to different values for each of you. Some of our core values related to money are reasonable, godly, and good. But some values may be tied to unhealthy or even sinful influences and behaviors. Figuring out what money represents to each of you is key to unlocking how you are being affected.

In many cases, one spouse leans toward being a spender and the other a saver. If you both happen to have the same bent, then you might end up either in huge debt or more like Ebenezer Scrooge. Extremes in direction may be problematic, so figuring that out together is critical.

Budget is a bad word to some folks, but the goal is to manage your money well and not let it manage you. Everyone needs a budget. And since it's your budget, you decide together how you want to set it up. You also need to decide which of you does a better job keeping up with the budget, paying bills, etc., and let them handle it.

Money is amoral. God allows us to have it to support our family, bless others, and expand his kingdom. The way we manage money is the issue, not the money itself. Conflict occurs when there is lack of clarity or unclear communication on what money means to each of you and how to manage it. This is an area where we can forge ahead in our growth as a couple if we are willing to hear the perspective of our spouse, ask questions, and seek to know their heart. Remember, we complement each other. As we explore our heads and our hearts in this area, we can weave a stronger unity.

> Whoever loves money never has enough; whoever loves wealth is never satisfied with their income. This too is meaningless. (Ecclesiastes 5:10 ESV)

> Keep your lives free from the love of money and be content with what you have, because God has said, "Never will I leave you; never will I forsake you." (Hebrews 13:5 ESV)

COUPLES ♥ CHALLENGE

♥ *What does money represent to you?*

♥ *How was money viewed, discussed, or used in your home growing up?*

♥ *Do you have a budget? If not, take steps to start one. (Budget forms can be found online.)*

♥ *If your spouse has a different perspective on money, what is something you can glean from them?*

♥ *If money has been a source of conflict for you as a couple, discuss how your differing perspectives or attitudes about money may have led to the conflict. Determine how you can factor in each perspective as you move forward.*

CONFLICT – WHAT'S YOUR PRIORITY?

> *Did he not make them one, with a portion of the Spirit in their union? And what was the one God seeking? Godly offspring. So, guard yourselves in your spirit, and let none of you be faithless to the wife of your youth.*
>
> **Malachi 2:15 ESV**

How busy are you and your family? Do you think you're above or below average? Here are five statistics to consider. The average American has less than twenty-six minutes of free time each day. The average employee works forty-seven to forty-nine hours a week. Forty percent of managers work more than sixty hours a week. Sixty-five percent of students are stressed because of their schedules. And finally, families only eat about 50 percent of their dinners together. [6]

---

6   U.S. Bureau of Labor Statistics, *American Time Use Survey 2022*

Does any of that sound like you? And with all of this in mind, how do you prioritize your marriage but also meet the demands of your careers, children, and everything else in life?

One of the few true equalizers in life is that we all get the same amount of time each day. We may not all get the same number of years, but the hours we each have in a day are the same. What we do with those hours can make a tremendous difference in the health and flourishing of our marriages.

So, how do you use this potential conflict to forge a stronger marriage?

- Decide that your marriage is the priority.

- Determine to make decisions about work and life through this filter.

- Know that this may mean saying no to some good things so you can say yes to the better things.

- If times of separation are required, limit these whenever possible.

- When this is not possible, realize that you must put some safe barriers in place to protect your relationship.

- Understand that open, honest communication is essential to navigating the marriage/work balance.

- Know that there will be seasons in your life that require conflicting schedules, but be mindful of how long these seasons last.

The bottom line for all of us is that we find time for what we think is important! That's why it's painful when we choose everything else over our spouse. When our marriage is not the priority, or one of us feels less significant than anything else, that's when we need to take heed. We were designed to be a helpmate for and to complement each other in having dominion over our world (the piece of it that God gives us); we share this together. If we lose this focus as our priority, conflicts occur.

Marriage is forged as we experience life together. That doesn't mean there must be a certain number of hours or days together, but it does mean that we figure out how to carve out time that preserves our unity and keeps our relationship a priority. This will look different for every couple. When a couple makes each other a priority, then time apart can build and increase their desire for one another.

Keeping your marriage a priority will not be easy, as everything else in life will scream for your attention and time. Navigating this requires wisdom, discussion, negotiation, and a willingness to make hard choices. The tyranny of the urgent always competes with the important. For your marriage to flourish and be all you want it to be, it must remain more important than the other things.

> Likewise, husbands live with your wives in an understanding way, showing honor to the woman as the weaker vessel, since they are heirs with you of the grace of life, so that your prayers may not be hindered. (1 Peter 3:7 ESV)

> Above all, keep loving one another earnestly, since love covers a multitude of sins. (1 Peter 4:8 ESV)

COUPLES ♥ CHALLENGE

♥ *Do you think your marriage is the top priority for you?*

♥ *If not, what changed? What has become the priority?*

♥ *What is one action you can take to move toward making your marriage the top priority?*

♥ *Schedule a day and time to talk about your schedules. What hard choices or creative ideas do you need to make so your marriage is the priority?*

WEEK 37

CONFLICT – THEY ARE YOUR KIDS!

> *Train up a child in the way they should go, and even when they are old, they will not turn from it.*
>
> **Proverbs 22:6 ESV**

Parenting can create conflict in our marriage because it opens a whole new world of decisions to navigate. How many kids should we have? How should we space them? What about our careers? Should one of us stay home, or do we both continue to work? What boundaries do we set for them? How strict should the discipline be? What kind of parents do we want to be? The list could go on and on.

All these questions and decisions point to our core beliefs and expectations around parenting. Some of these likely were not discussed prior to having children. Even if they were, an intellectual discussion around parenting and the actual parenting can be miles apart. What sounded reasonable before those precious little people showed up may now feel more difficult or not the right course.

Conflicts can come from disagreements on parenting decisions. We each should be able to share from our perspective what and why we think a certain path is wisest. We may not ever entirely agree on all aspects of parenting, but we always want our marriage and parenting to have a united front.

Another thing that creates conflict is when our children, not our marriage, become the focus and priority of our lives. It is easy for this to happen. At the beginning they are so small and dependent on us for everything. They demand what they want and need, and they have no patience. Even as they get bigger, the challenge is to not allow our marriage to become kid focused, but to remain couple focused.

Our children are a gift to us on loan from God. We are to teach them, train them, and then let them go. We can't set aside our marriage for twenty years or so while we are parenting and then expect there to be something left when the children are gone. The interesting thing is that God designed it so a marriage that stays couple centered and not kid centered teaches essential truths to our children:

- They are not the center of the world.

- They are a part of our family, not the totality.

- Our marriage is the most important thing.

- Our marriage commitment provides them with a strong and secure foundation.

So, if you want to do the best for your children, keep your marriage a priority. Let them see a mom and dad who demonstrate the gospel through a marriage that reflects God's covenant love for his bride. May I press in on this a little more and say that even your married adult children need this. They want to see their parents have a fulfilling marriage, and they want them to stay together. They want the example and encouragement of your marriage that says they can make it in their marriage as well.

> Children are a gift from the Lord; they are a reward from him. (Psalm 127:3 NLT)

> Children's children are the crown to the aged, and parents are the pride of their children. (Proverbs 17:6 NIV)

> Trust in the LORD with all your heart and do not lean on your own understanding. In all your ways acknowledge Him, and He will make your paths straight. (Proverbs 3:5–6 NASB)

COUPLES ♥ CHALLENGE

♥ *Rate your marriage on a scale of 1–10, with 1 = child centered and 10 = couple centered.*

♥ *Is this where you want to be?*

♥ *Are there habits you had in place before you had children that you have stopped? Can you restart them?*

♥ *What is one thing you can start doing that will help your marriage remain, or become, more couple centered?*

DANGER! LANDMINES IN THE AREA!

He that trusted in his own heart is a fool; but whoso walks wisely, he shall be delivered.

Proverbs 28:26 KJV

Did you know that there are over 100 million landmines estimated to be buried around the globe? In Israel, you can see areas with barbed wire that have *Danger/Do Not Enter* signs indicating areas where there are possible landmines. I would think that if someone sees the danger sign that indicates landmines, they will not walk in that area. But what about when there are no signs?

Humans can sometimes have landmines buried deep inside us too. We may not even realize they are there. And what happens when our spouse steps on one of the landmines buried inside us? Well, there's probably going to be an ugly explosion. We may feel this deep, painful response to something our spouse has done or said. Our response is based on the "feeling" that a landmine was just triggered inside us. Often, the response is exaggerated based on our internal alarms going off.

Our spouse may not even know there was a landmine. They may not know this is an area that needs some caution/warning signs. They may have no idea that they have wandered into a restricted area that is vulnerable and dangerous. They have shrapnel bombarding them, yet they have no idea what just happened.

These landmines are left over from earlier wounds, painful experiences, traumatic events, or a lifetime of negative, untrue beliefs. The challenge is to identify and acknowledge them. Once we can expose the wound, we can start to move toward healing.

We need our marriage to be a safe, unveiled place where we can share about our landmines. This is critical for several reasons:

- If we don't know our spouse has these landmines, we are likely to step on them.

- Even knowing there are landmines does not mean we will never set one off.

- Realizing that we may have stepped on a landmine can give us empathy to understand that the reaction is based on the painful response our spouse feels.

- It may appear that the explosion is toward us, but recognizing that we may have reopened past painful wounds can help us give grace to our spouse.

Learning how to manage the landmines in our marriage is crucial. If we don't, the tendency is to stay in a warfare mode. Landmines are tripped, explosions occur, and painful shrapnel wounds us. We respond with defensiveness, anger, bitterness, or other hurtful responses that many times set off more landmines.

Just like it is not possible to remove all the landmines around the world, it may not be possible to remove every landmine inside us. The more we become aware of our landmines, share them with our spouse, and acknowledge that these are areas that need careful treading, the more we can avoid triggering one. This is a place in our marriage where we need to honor and cherish each other by tenderly avoiding the landmines whenever we can.

> Be kind to one another, tenderhearted, forgiving one another, as God in Christ forgave you. (Ephesians 4:32 ESV)

> Let us then with confidence draw near to the throne of grace, that we may receive mercy and find grace to help in our time of need. (Hebrews 4:16 ESV)

COUPLES ♥ CHALLENGE

♥ *Discuss whether you have ever hit a landmine in your spouse.*

♥ *Does your spouse agree that it is a landmine?*

♥ *Are you able to talk about where you think it comes from?*

♥ *Can you devise some parameters around how to not trip your landmines?*

♥ *Are there landmines in you and/or your spouse that can be removed?*

STAY S.A.F.E.

> *A tender answer turns away rage, but a prickly reply spikes anger. The words of the wise extend knowledge, but foolish people utter nonsense. The Eternal can see all things; His gaze is fixed on both the evil and the good. A word of encouragement heals the one who receives it, but a deceitful word breaks the spirit.*
>
> **Proverbs 15:1–4 VOICE**

While conflict in marriage may be inevitable, we can approach it in a way that it can strengthen the marriage rather than damage it. If we let our emotions take over, damage often follows. Anger, fear, and other emotions can lead us to say things that attack the person rather than focus on the issue that created the conflict.

Scripture speaks about the power of the tongue. James 3:9 warns us that we can both bless and curse with the same tongue. But with the power of the Holy Spirit, we can learn to control what we say when dealing with conflict.

We know that to build deep intimacy in marriage, we need to feel safe to express our needs, feelings, disappointments, and desires. When we express those things in a harsh or critical way, our spouse often gets defensive or lashes back at us. So, how can we express ourselves in a way that doesn't come across as harsh, critical, or accusatory?

A game-changer for us was when we started using the S.A.F.E. Method, which is a powerful tool that can help avoid explosive conflicts.

"S" is for situation.

What is the *situation* that makes you feel fearful, neglected, ignored, unseen or heard?

"A" is for action.

When the above situation occurs, what is the action your spouse has taken to create the feelings you are experiencing?

"F" is for feelings.

A situation arises, your spouse acts, and these feelings are your response.

"E" is for empathy.

The goal of the S.A.F.E. Method is for your spouse to understand how their actions have made you feel.

Here is a situation to consider. You have come home from a two-day work trip. Your spouse is watching TV, and you come in excited to see them and announce, "Honey, I'm home!" No response. They continue to watch TV. How does that make you feel? How should you respond? Anger? Criticism? Nothing?

Let's set this up:

- Situation: When you have been away from your spouse.

- Action: Instead of welcoming you with a hug or kiss, your spouse ignores you.

- Feeling: The lack of response from your spouse makes you feel _____.

- Empathy: How can you help them understand how you feel without attacking them?

Carla is great at doing this with me. Instead of yelling at me or criticizing me, she will come and say, "Johnny, when I walked in and you didn't even acknowledge I was home, it made me feel unvalued. It made me think you don't care whether I came home or not." She doesn't attack me, so I have nothing to be defensive about. Instead, I think about how I would feel if the situation was reversed. I can empathize with her feelings, and I feel convicted and moved to apologize and ask for her forgiveness.

Will your spouse always respond the way you want them to? Probably not. Even so, let the Holy Spirit do his work. He is the only one who can change our hearts. But if we can move away from sniping and criticizing, as we often do when these situations happen, over time I believe we will see less conflict and more growth in our marriage. I can confirm that using the S.A.F.E. Method has impacted our marriage in a healthy way. It works!

Don't say anything that would hurt another person. Instead, speak only what is good so that you can give help wherever it is needed. That way, what you say will help those who hear you. (Ephesians 4:29 NOG)

Sharp words cut like a sword, but words of wisdom heal. (Proverbs 12:18 CEV)

COUPLES ♥ CHALLENGE

♥ *Take some time together to reflect on past situations and conflicts that you could have used the S.A.F.E. Method to deal with. How might it have looked different if you'd done so?*

♥ *This week, look for an opportunity to practice the S.A.F.E. Method. Try to make it a habit in the weeks ahead.*

THE SEASONS OF MARRIAGE

For everything there is a season, and a time for every matter under heaven: a time to be born, and a time to die; a time to plant, and a time to pluck up what is planted; a time to kill, and a time to heal; a time to break down, and a time to build up; a time to weep, and a time to laugh; a time to mourn, and a time to dance; a time to cast away stones, and a time to gather stones together; a time to embrace, and a time to refrain from embracing; a time to seek, and a time to lose; a time to keep, and a time to cast away; a time to tear, and a time to sew; a time to keep silence, and a time to speak; a time to love, and a time to hate; a time for war, and a time for peace.

Ecclesiastes 3:1–8 ESV

According to climatologists, the Canary Islands have the best climate of any place in the world. The lowest temperature for the year is 64 degrees in February and the highest is 77 degrees in August. It is spring all year long. Some people might like that weather all the time, but I enjoy all the seasons. The flowers of spring. The long days of summer. The first cool morning of fall and the changing leaves the season brings. The beauty of fresh snow in winter when everything is transformed and looks clean and white.

Just as there are changing seasons throughout the year, marriage has its own seasons. What do those seasons look like? This week we will look at an overview of each one. In the weeks ahead, we will take a more in-depth look at each of those seasons.

Spring is a season of hope and anticipation. New things are on the horizon. There's excitement in the relationship, and possibilities abound. *Spring* can come to a marriage when you are just beginning your life together or anytime along the way.

The vitality of *Summer* is when life is bustling. *Summer* is often fast-paced, when the goals and dreams of *Spring* are coming to fruition. It is the sweet spot of marriage.

Fall is often a transitional time. It can be a time for reflection and recalibration of life, and a time to take heed of the relational warning signs and act before *Winter* takes hold.

Winter is a barren season. Dreams have died, and relationships are cold and struggling. It's usually the most difficult season to navigate. In the depths of *Winter*, it may seem that *Spring* will never come again.

Whatever season you find yourself in right now, here are some key points to remember:

- The seasons of marriage are a cyclical journey, with couples moving in and out of seasons, but not necessarily in order.

- Every couple is unique, and how they experience the seasons will be unique as well.

- Spouses may see themselves in a different season. One spouse's *Summer* can be the other spouse's *Fall*.

- Your own personal season can impact the marriage relationship. If one spouse is in the darkness of *Winter* personally, it will likely push the marriage into a different season.

- Most couples will experience each of the four seasons sometime in their marriage.

In life, if you don't like the seasons where you live, you can move somewhere else. Perhaps you want the year-round spring of the Canary Islands. You have a choice in marriage as well. You can do the things that keep your marriage in the sweet spot of *Spring* and *Summer*. Even in the most difficult circumstances, you can experience a healthy, vibrant season of marriage.

> And we know that for those who love God all things work together for good, for those who are called according to his purpose. (Romans 8:28 ESV)

> Yet I am confident I will see the LORD'S goodness while I am here in the land of the living. Wait patiently for the LORD. Be brave and courageous. Yes, wait patiently for the LORD. (Psalm 27:13–14 NLT)

COUPLES ♥ CHALLENGE

♥ *Look at the following groups of words. Focusing on your relationship right now, which group of words most resonates with you?*

> *Critical, angry, hopeless, withdrawn, resentful*
>
> *Satisfying, peaceful, content, supportive, teamwork*
>
> *Uncertain, frustrated, tired, drifting, stressful*
>
> *Exciting, hopeful, joyful, anticipating, growing*

Share with each other the group of words you chose, and explain why you chose that group. Were you in agreement with each other? If not, discuss your differences.

THE SEASON OF SPRING

Lazy farmers don't plow when they should;
they expect a harvest, but there is none.

Proverbs 20:4 NLT

Spring is the time of plans and projects.

Leo Tolstoy

*S*pring is the season of hope when new things are on the horizon, a time of excitement and anticipation. We often think of just those first years of marriage as the *Spring*, but marriage can be full of *Springs*. Anything that is new to your marriage can be a springboard into the excitement of *Spring*— expecting a child, moving to a new house or city, a new job, or a transition of family such as the kids heading to college. All of these are times of hope and expectation that characterize *Spring*.

The emotions of *Spring* include joy, romance, excitement, and fun, to name a few. This is a happy time. Enjoy it to the fullest. *Spring* usually brings a mindset of optimism, trust, and expectations, and those mindsets lead to the behaviors of teamwork, sharing of ideas, and planning together, along with effective communication as new things are on the horizon. The key to *Spring* is knowing how to leverage the season for the benefit of your marriage.

When Jesus took his disciples to the area in Israel now known as Bania, he asked them who they thought he was. Peter answered, "You are the Christ, the Son of the living God" (Matthew 16:16 ESV). Jesus went on to say that this truth was the foundation that the disciples would build the church upon. The birth of Christianity started on a solid foundation. In marriage, *Spring* is a time to build and shore up your foundation. How is your foundation?

We often think of spring as the time we get our yards and gardens ready. We prepare the soil. We add fertilizer. We plant. We do what we can do to enjoy the coming summer and reap a harvest. The same thing applies to our marriage, whether it's just starting out or anytime the season of *Spring* comes around. Intentionality in *Spring* leads to a long season of *Summer*, even when there are storms or drought. Foundational preparation is key. We always encourage couples to build and strengthen the marriage foundations when things are good.

So, what are the foundational principles to work on?

- Focus on planting for a spiritual harvest in your marriage.

- Build focused, daily communication patterns.

- Keep pursuing and romancing.

- Keep developing key relational skills, including clear communication skills and healthy conflict resolution.

Spring is an exciting time to not only plan for the new, but also to check each of these foundational principles for your marriage. Where do things look good? Are there areas that need repair or freshening up? What are some new things to add to the garden of your marriage? The *Spring* seasons of marriage are some of the most delightful. Take advantage of Spring not just to prepare for the new, but to also strengthen and beautify what is already there.

> But forget all that—it is nothing compared to what I am going to do. For I am about to do something new. See, I have already begun! Do you not see it? I will make a pathway through the wilderness. I will create rivers in the dry wasteland. (Isaiah 43:18–19 NLT)

> "Excellence is never an accident. It is always the result of high intention, sincere effort, and intelligent execution; it represents the wise choice of many alternatives—choice, not chance, determines your destiny." (Anonymous)

COUPLES ♥ CHALLENGE

♥ *Set up a date night and take time to review your vision for marriage (Week 14). The changes of* Spring *may be a wonderful time to revise the vision.*

♥ *Draw up a list of three things you want more of in your marriage. Plan a to talk about your list and exactly what those three things look like to you. Create a plan and put it into action.*

♥ *Choose an informative book on growing spiritually that you can read and discuss together.*

THE SEASON OF SUMMER

> *And now, just as you accepted Christ Jesus as your Lord, you must continue to follow him. Let your roots grow down into him, and let your lives be built on him. Then your faith will grow strong in the truth you were taught, and you will overflow with thankfulness.*
>
> **Colossians 2:6–7 NLT**

We live in Georgia, and as spring moves into summer, our area can get some incredible thunderstorms. For those who are smart and stay under cover, the storms can be spectacular to watch as they light up the night sky. The storms can also be destructive, as I witnessed when lightning hit a tree in our front yard. I heard the bolt hit and opened my front door to see what it hit. The sugar maple in our front yard looked like it had exploded. Pieces were scattered everywhere. The tree went from fifty feet tall to a smoldering stump in an instant. In the days ahead we cleaned up the debris, cut the stump to ground level, and assumed the tree was done. Were we ever wrong!

Evidently, that sugar maple had deep roots and wasn't ready to call it quits. In the days ahead we saw new growth. Today, it's bigger and fuller than it ever was before the lightning delivered what we thought was a death blow. Strong roots will do that. That's what *Summers* are for, giving your marriage strong roots to survive the storms.

If the season of *Spring* is a time of planning and new things in life and marriage, then *Summer* is the sweet spot that allows the roots to grow deep and strong. *Summer* is about the fulfillment of plans made in *Spring*. It is living a life of abundance in what God has given you—the season you want to live in as much as possible.

Summer is a season of contentment but not inactivity. To prolong this season, keep the intentionality going. Your marriage is in a healthy place, but keep pushing toward a deeper intimacy and maturity spiritually, emotionally, and physically. In *Summer*, you get to enjoy the fruits of what you sowed in *Spring*.

The emotions of *Summer* include satisfaction, fulfillment, mutual enjoyment, and fun. The mindset includes positivity and deep commitment to each other, along with trust and intentionality. Your marriage is a priority! *Summer* is also an active season. When weeds raise their ugly head, we deal with them before they take over the yard. When the weeds of marriage crop up, deal with them then. Don't let them grow into something bigger. Keep watering and fertilizing your marriage to maintain its health. If you stop being intentional, you start to drift and you may find yourself moving into a season of *Fall*.

Every season of marriage has challenges. If you build a sturdy foundation, practice good communication skills, and handle conflict in a healthy way, you can keep the relationship from moving into the harder seasons of *Fall* and *Winter*. *Summer* is an easy time to get lazy and coast—don't! Follow through with building the vision you created in *Spring*. Keep moving toward your goals and adjust when necessary.

Here are some keys to extending *Summer*:

- **Strong communication is important.**
  - Connect daily, even if briefly. Share your highs and lows of each day.
  - Set aside longer talk times to focus on each other.

- **Date nights are a priority.**
  - Schedule your date nights to ensure they happen.
  - If something comes up, reschedule.

- **Keep the Love Tank full and ready to go.**
  - Express love to your spouse the way they need it.
  - Know that daily expressions of love are more important than occasional big gestures.

- **Forge ahead with conflict.**
  - Deal with issues when they start. Don't let the ashes of unresolved conflict smother the flames of love.
  - Practice "withholds" to keep conflicts in check (keep reading for information about withholds).
  - Remember, conflict is an opportunity to forge a strong marriage.

Summer is the time to build deep roots in your marriage. The big difference between *Spring* and *Summer* are the deep roots you build together.

> You can't find firm footing in a swamp, but life rooted in God stands firm. (Proverbs 12:3 MSG)

COUPLES ♥ CHALLENGE

♥ *Build spiritual intimacy in your marriage.*

   Pray together at least weekly.

   Find a place to serve together.

   Keep reading and discussing the book you chose.

   Ask each other the 5 Questions weekly (Week 16).

♥ *Practice your "withholds."*

♥ ♥ ♥ ♥ ♥ ♥ ♥ ♥ ♥ ♥ ♥ ♥ ♥

Withholds: A Proactive Way to Deal with Conflict[7]

Withholds happen every day between spouses. They are "things" that aren't "addressed," not due to you not wanting to but because of the speed at which people do life. Withholds can be positive or negative.

POSITIVE WITHHOLDS

- You think of a positive thought, comment, or feeling about your spouse but never say it.

    - "She really looks good tonight."

    - "I need to thank him for picking up dinner on the way home."

    - "I appreciate the way she/he handled that with the kids."

NEGATIVE WITHHOLDS

- Something occurs that upsets you, offends you, or irritates you, but in the moment you can't say it. (The problem is that negative withholds always show up later; they will come out at some point.)

    - You're out to dinner with friends and your spouse says something that feels critical, but you don't say anything.

HANDLING WITHHOLDS

- Once a week, take time to share any withholds. Even if there are no negatives, share the positives.

- Take turns, one person at a time.

- Share in a 2:1 ratio of positives to negatives. If there is a negative withhold to share, there must be positives shared as well.

- The listener can only respond with "Thank you."

- Neither can respond to a negative withhold for at least thirty minutes.

♥ ♥ ♥ ♥ ♥ ♥ ♥ ♥ ♥ ♥ ♥ ♥ ♥

---

7   Drs. Les & Leslie Parrott, *The Good Fight: How Conflict Can Bring You Closer* (Franklin, TN: Worthy, 2013), 68-70.

THE SEASON OF FALL

> *And in the morning, if the sky is dark and red,*
> *you say that it will be a rainy day. These are signs*
> *of the weather. You see these signs in the sky and*
> *know what they mean. In the same way, you see*
> *the things that are happening now. These are also*
> *signs, but you don't know their meaning.*
>
> **Matthew 16:3 ERV**

Of all the seasons of the year, fall may be my favorite. I love that first crisp, cool morning after a sweltering summer. As the days become shorter, the brilliant hues of turning leaves shine in all their glory. Soon those same leaves will form a carpet on the ground. The world is moving toward winter.

While fall may be a beautiful season in the calendar year, the season of *Fall* in marriage is a time of warning. We prefer to live in a perpetual *Spring* or *Summer* in marriage, and if we're not attentive, *Fall* will slowly creep up on us. Heed the warning signs if you don't want to find yourself in the coldness of *Winter*. The emotions that signal an approaching *Fall* are feelings of coolness in the relationship, feeling dissatisfaction, and feeling underappreciated or ignored. There may be increased anxiety about the relationship or even a growing resentfulness.

While *Spring* and *Summer* carry the mindsets of positivity and teamwork, *Fall's* mindsets are characterized by a focus on negatives, frustration, and blaming. As *Fall* deepens, we find ourselves disconnected and drifting apart. We disengage, ignoring the warning signs and often burying ourselves in the busyness of life. We must wake up before we plunge into the depths of *Winter*! Ignoring the signs is like letting the leaves pile up and ignoring them. Whatever is beneath may soon die if not attended to.

Years ago, we had drifted into a *Fall* season. Life was hard and stressful, and we were not being intentional about our marriage. We allowed life to be in charge, and our marriage stopped being a priority. I (Johnny) would not have said that our marriage wasn't important, but I was not doing anything that proved it was. Carla was trying to tell me how lost, unseen, and unimportant she felt, but I was missing all the signs. Interestingly, God used another believer—one Carla did not even know that well—to ask her a question about us and our relationship. She felt like she'd had cold water thrown in her face. Carla will say to this day that it was a huge wake-up call to realizing we were in a *Fall* season.

Couples usually find themselves in the season of *Fall* because they have stopped making their marriage their priority. Life gets in the way and the focus moves away from the relationship. The apostle Peter told us that Satan prowls around like a hungry lion

(1 Peter 5:8). Know that Satan hates marriage and will seek to distract you with the concerns of life. Don't let him! The longer your attention is diverted from the health of your marriage, the harder it will be to get back to a season of *Spring* or *Summer*.

So, what can you do?

Be vigilant. As soon as you feel the drift begin, correct your course. Set a date night. Double up on communication. Go back to the habits of *Spring* and *Summer* with a renewed focus. Don't be afraid to get help from a marriage coach or mentor. Don't let pride get in the way. Pride can be one of the big barriers to growing and keeping intimacy. Create a plan together and put it into action!

> I have told you all this so that you may have peace in me. Here on earth, you will have many trials and sorrows. But take heart because I have overcome the world. (John 16:33 NLT)

> Pride comes before destruction, and an arrogant spirit before a fall. (Proverbs 16:18 HCSB)

COUPLES ♥ CHALLENGE

Take time this week to do a quick check-up on your marriage by answering the following questions individually and then discussing your answers.

♥ *Are we being intentional with our marriage and keeping it the priority?*

♥ *Our last date night was* _____.

♥ *On a scale of 1–5, with 1 being poor and 5 being awesome, our communication is mostly at level* _____.

♥ *On a scale of 1–5, with 1 being distant and 5 being very close, how would you rate your intimacy levels?*

    Spiritual _____

    Emotional _____

    Physical _____

♥ *Do you have any sense that things in your marriage are not healthy? What aspects, if any, give you concern? Trust your intuition. Take action.*

THE SEASON OF WINTER

Hear my cry, O God, listen to my prayer; from the end of the earth, I call to you when my heart is faint. Lead me to the rock that is higher than I, for you have been my refuge, a strong tower against the enemy.

Psalm 61:1–3 ESV

For there is hope for a tree, when it is cut down, that it will sprout again, and its shoots will not fail. Though its roots grow old in the ground and its stump dies in the dry soil, at the scent of water it will flourish and put forth sprigs like a plant.

Job 14:7–9 NASB

In the fantasy series *Game of Thrones*, the saying "Winter is coming" is a harbinger of hard times ahead. When we consider the season of *Winter* in marriage, we are not thinking of a beautiful, gentle snowfall and all the world looking clean and white, but a season of challenging times. Winter in marriage can be a harsh, stark, barren wasteland where the relationship is cold, dispassionate, and on the verge of death—a season that no one wants to experience. It may come about because of an extreme wound or from years of neglect. When couples neglect the warning signs of *Fall*, a season of *Winter* often sets in.

Some of the emotions of *Winter* include hopelessness, despair, anger, bitterness, and deep hurt. These emotions lead to a mindset of rigidity. We refuse to move from our position. We may have a myopic view that says there is nothing good to be found in the relationship. Everything is wretched. Couples are often critical and demeaning during this season. If couples are speaking at all to each other, their words are often harsh and wounding. They have withdrawn from each other emotionally and physically. By this point, there is a good chance that one or both are looking for a way out. The good thing is with God there is always hope (Job 13:15).

Now, if you find yourself in a season of *Winter*, or maybe you have someone close to you in that hard season, you're probably wondering what you can do. There are both things to do and things to avoid.

First, let's look at some things to avoid. Stay away from what John Gottman (gottman.com) calls "The 4 Horsemen."[8] These

---

8   https://www.gottman.com/blog/the-four-horsemen-recognizing-criticism-contempt-defensiveness-and-stonewalling/

behaviors left unchecked can kill a marriage, especially one in a struggling situation. They are

- **Criticism** – This is attacking the other person instead of focusing on the behavior. We are saying that they are defective.

- **Defensiveness** – We play the victim. It is never our fault. We want to deflect from any responsibility for the situation.

- **Contempt** – We seek to hurt, humiliate, and disrespect someone. According to John Gottman, this is the number one indicator of divorce.

- **Stonewalling** – We shut down and refuse to respond to our spouse.

Now, I wish I could say that we have never been in *Winter*, but we have—several times, in fact. We felt unable to move forward and stop the cycle of unresolved hurt and repeating conflicts. We were stuck, only able to see what was not working, what we did not like, and what made us frustrated. But we did not want to stay there; we wanted help. We wanted to go back to a season of *Spring*.

So, what do you do if you find yourself in the season of *Winter*? GET HELP. Most couples are going to need rescuing when in the clutches of *Winter*. It's usually not something they can dig themselves out of alone. Find a good marriage counselor or marriage coach. Don't get stuck. Doing nothing usually ends in more pain and heartache. Healing is possible, and we are proof of that.

> For there is hope for a tree, when it is cut down, that it will sprout again, and its shoots will not fail. Though its roots grow old in the ground and its stump dies in the dry soil, at the scent of water it will flourish and put forth sprigs like a plant. (Job 14:7–9 ESV)

COUPLES ♥ CHALLENGE

♥ *As you think back over the last weeks of the seasons of marriage, in what season would you put your marriage right now?*

♥ *If you are in* Spring *or* Summer, *brainstorm steps to stay there. Are you being intentional about your marriage?*

♥ *If there are warning signs, what are they? What is the root issue? Devise a plan to deal with it. Schedule an appointment with a marriage coach or counselor.*

WHEN THE WINE RUNS OUT

> *The wine supply ran out during the festivities,*
> *so Jesus' mother told him, "They have no*
> *more wine." ... His mother told the servants,*
> *"Do whatever he tells you."*
>
> ### John 2:3, 5 NLT

I love that the first miracle that Jesus performed occurred at a wedding. I also love the exchange between Jesus and his mother. After she told him that the wine had run out, Jesus responded that his time had not come yet. Don't you wonder how she might have looked at him? What did her nonverbal cues say to him? Whatever it was, her response to the servants was, "Do whatever he tells you" (John 2:5 NLT).

There are times in marriage when it seems the wine has run out and we feel empty. We don't know what to do. This is when we need to do what Jesus's mother said to the servants—do whatever Jesus tells us to do.

And what did Jesus tell them to do? He told the servants, "Fill the jars with water" (John 2:7 ESV). So they filled them. Likewise, we need to do what Jesus has told us, which is that he has given us his Word filled with how we are to treat and respond to one another. Maybe we need to say less, pray more, examine our own hearts to see what part of the marriage issues we need to own, and respond in kindness even when we don't feel it. We need to choose to act in love. We can only do what we can do.

While we do that, we wait to see what Jesus will do. The servants did what they were told even though they had no idea what would happen. It did not look promising to just fill the jars with water, and sometimes our marriage may not look like anything can fill it up or fix the problems. But we don't know what God may do. We can only act on what he has told us to do.

We so yearn and crave the miracle. It's hard to just do the other things that Scripture tells us to do. These things may seem ridiculous, not practical, not helpful, or even a waste of our time. So we must choose to do what God has shown us, even when we don't know the outcome. The miracle may or may not look as we thought. However, God working in our heart and changing us is the miracle!

> Jesus said to the servants, "Fill the jars with water" so they filled them to the brim. (John 2:7 NIV)

> Do not merely listen to the word, and so deceive yourselves. Do what it says. (James 1:22 NIV)

COUPLES ♥ CHALLENGE

♥ *If you could change one thing about your marriage right now, what would it be? Why that one thing? What difference could there be if it changes?*

♥ *Discuss how you can start to make that change.*

♥ *Is there anything that the Bible says you should be doing in your marriage but you're not doing it right now? If so, why not?*

FORGIVENESS

Forgiveness is applying the blood of Jesus to every wound I have received or ever will receive.

Bruce Hebel

Get rid of all bitterness, rage, anger, harsh words, and slander, as well as all types of evil behavior. Instead, be kind to each other, tenderhearted, forgiving one another, just as God through Christ has forgiven you.

Ephesians 4:31–32 NLT

We have all been there—an unkind word, a sharp retort, emotional or physical abuse, emotional or physical betrayal. Someone has deeply wounded us and we can't get over it. We try to let it go but we can't. And why should we? They hurt us and should pay for it. So, we hold on to the hurt. We nurture the anger. It feels good—for a while. But if we stay there, bitterness begins to take over and the relationship starts to die. Regardless of the details, there is good news that is foundational to our faith—the blessing of forgiveness.

Marriage is a forge in which God transforms us into the image of Christ. As the apostle Paul tells us, we forgive those who hurt us because God has forgiven us (Ephesians 4:32). How can we not extend that same forgiveness to others? But depending on the depth of the hurt, we can struggle to extend forgiveness to those who wound us, especially when it's our spouse. Forgiveness can be costly because we give up our rights to revenge and retribution. Forgiveness means we stop trying to change the one who has hurt us and allow God to change their heart.

Like love, forgiveness is active, not passive. We choose to discontinue brooding about the offense, knowing that to do so will allow bitterness to take over. We choose not to keep bringing it up to our spouse and holding it over their head. We choose not to talk about the offense with others if they are not part of the problem or the solution. Every day, we choose to act toward our spouse the way that God chooses to act toward us. Remembering the empty wine jars, we do what God tells us to do, and in this case that is to forgive.

Sometimes we struggle with the myths of forgiveness. We think we must forget what someone did to us in order to forgive. We can never forget those deep hurts, but they can become markers we can look back on and marvel at the grace that God gives us. Now, what if we don't feel like offering forgiveness? Does that mean it is fake? To this we say, forgiveness is an act of obedience. God is concerned about our obedience, not our feelings. Feeling often follows when we act in obedience.

Forgiveness is not always easy to extend, but it is right to do so. When Jesus was asked how many times we have to forgive others, his answer was an unlimited number of times (see Matthew 18:21–22). If we want to build a strong, healthy marriage that lasts, we will need to learn to forgive our spouse when they let us down and hurt us. Forgiveness sets us free from the bondage that anger and bitterness bring. It's what is best for the relationship and, above all, it honors God. This quote by Gary Rosberg sums it up beautifully:

> Forgiveness is how you bring your relationship into the light. It's how you set free the offended and the offender and allow for reconciliation. In fact, the benefits of forgiveness are so overwhelming that if you cannot forgive for the sake of your spouse, you will want to forgive for how it will benefit you alone. Your choice is to let go of the wrongs done against you or to pay a heavy personal price. God says you must forgive— because he has forgiven you.[9]

> Get rid of all bitterness, rage, anger, harsh words, and slander, as well as all types of evil behavior. Instead, be kind to each other, tenderhearted, forgiving one another, just as God through Christ has forgiven you. (Ephesians 4:31–32 NLT)

---

9   "The Myths of Forgiveness," The Rosbergs, February 25, 2020, https://www.americasfamilycoaches.com/blog/2020/2/25/the-myths-of-forgiveness.

COUPLES ♥ CHALLENGE

♥ *Time for reflection. Are there any past offenses or hurts you continue to hold? Anything for which you have not forgiven your spouse or someone else? Make a list.*

♥ *What are the barriers that keep you from forgiving?*

♥ *Spend time with God this week and release those things to him. See yourself releasing them from your hand and giving them up. Ask God to empower you to be obedient and forgive.*

♥ *If you are struggling with forgiving, check out www.forgivingforward.com for help.*

DO YOU WANT TO BE HEALED?

> *When Jesus saw him lying there and knew that he had already been there a long time, he said to him, "Do you want to be healed?"*
>
> **John 5:6 ESV**

In the scene from *The Chosen* where Jesus is getting ready to heal the paralytic, he first asked him, "Do you want to be healed?" The man started making excuses about why he couldn't get into the water. Jesus said to him again, "Do you want to be healed?"

We can make all the excuses in the world, but the question is still the same. Do we want to be healed? It seems like a crazy question, but if our marriage is hurt or sick, do we want healing? Now, I'm not talking about a miracle where in a split second the healing occurs, like in the Scripture above. I mean the kind that requires a willingness to confront hard issues, allow God to show us our part in the problem, and possibly get assistance through coaching or counseling.

If you had a disease that needed intense medical treatments but had side effects that were going to be incredibly difficult, would you do it for the chance of a remission or cure? The answer probably depends on multiple factors. But many people will put themselves through extremely challenging treatments for the small chance that it will result in a positive outcome. Sadly, when it comes to giving the same kind of effort for experiencing soul-wrenching arduous work to save, restore, or renew our marriage, many say it is too much, too hard, or just not worth it.

May I push in on this and challenge you? Yes, it is worth doing the hard thing. Nothing worthwhile is ever easy. But it can be glorious. This may be the path to a renewed commitment, increased intimacy, and true delight.

Remember, our marriage is to image Christ's love for his bride, the church. We are to reflect that kind of love and covenant commitment. We are called to love each other not with the kind of momentary preference of what feels good, but with the other's good in mind. The "good" is defined by God, not us.

This may mean not pleasing ourselves but being willing to choose God's will over our own. We love each other with the mind of Christ for our spouse's eternal good, to build each other up in our faith. We are fueled to do this by knowing God's Word and his promises to give us endurance and allow us to take the harder road. His Word and his Spirit provide us comfort and enable us to be free from selfishness, all while genuinely loving one another.

We who are strong must be considerate of those who are

sensitive about things like this. We must not just please ourselves. We should help others do what is right and build them up in the Lord. (Romans 15:1–2 NLT)

Owe no one anything, except to love each other, for the one who loves another has fulfilled the law. (Romans 13:8 ESV)

COUPLES ♥ CHALLENGE

♥ *Are you willing to have an honest conversation with your spouse about the state of your marriage?*

♥ *Can you identify any area(s) that need healing?*

♥ *Are you willing to get whatever help is needed?*

♥ *If you are in a good place, how would you like to see your marriage grow?*

♥ *What is one thing you would like to be different in your marriage six months from now? Brainstorm steps you can take together to make that happen.*

FIRST THINGS FIRST

> *But I have this complaint against you. You don't love me or each other as you did at first!*
>
> ### Revelation 2:4 NLT

This verse is in the context of John writing his vision when he was exiled on the island of Patmos. This message was to the church at Ephesus, and it acknowledged everything they had done; they had persevered, enduring hard things and not growing weary. However, the message also had a rebuke: they had forsaken the love they had at first.

This message can speak to the heart of our personal walk with the Lord. We can be so busy doing so many things that we lose sight of what should be first. We forget and forsake the most important first thing—loving the Lord. Our activity can replace relationships. Even good works, such as ministry, can blind us to desiring the activity more than desiring intimacy with God.

This message can also speak about our marriage relationships, which are to image Christ and his love for the church, his bride. We can get so busy with life, with all the good and vital things, that we lose sight of our marriage. We forsake our marriage for other things, even if it is good.

In most cases this is not intentional. We don't plan to let our marriage slip. We don't intend to allow other things to take priority, but they can and will if we're not careful. We may never think of walking away, but have we let our marriage relationship slip from its rightful place in our heart and lives? We need to ask ourselves, *Am I doing the kind of things that I did in the beginning? Am I loving my spouse the way I did when it was brand new?*

Revelation 2:5 urges the church at Ephesus to realize how far they have fallen, and to repent. We may need to do the same in our marriage. Recognize where you are compared to where you were or where you want to be. Acknowledge that you have fallen, let things slip, and lost sight of what was most important. This is always the first step.

We had to take that step. Admitting we were not in a good place was hard. We were supposed to know better. At that point of our lives, we were in ministry, for heaven's sake! But for us and others, acknowledging the fall is necessary to move forward. Getting help is not weak, it is wise. God used marriage counseling to help us see things we had not been able to see. It was a door God used to help us move toward each other.

To repent means we change the way we think, which leads to a change in how we act. So, if your marriage is not going in the right direction, are you believing and thinking the way that God desires you to? Time for some soul searching. Have you lost the love and passion you first had in your marriage? Ask God to show you where your thinking does not match with his truth. Based on that truth, return to that first love.

> Consider how far you have fallen! Repent and do the things you did at first. (Revelation 2:5 NIV)

> But seek first the kingdom of God and his righteousness, and all these things will be added to you. (Matthew 6:33 ESV)

> For where your treasure is there will your heart be also. (Luke 12:34 ESV)

COUPLES ♥ CHALLENGE

♥ *Other than your relationship with God, is there anything that you see as a higher priority in your life than your marriage? If so, what is it?*

♥ *Write on a piece of paper how you would rate your marriage being the priority in your life. Use a scale of 1–10, with 1 = low priority and 10 = high priority.*

♥ *Share your numbers. Do they surprise you? Are you in agreement, or do you see it differently?*

♥ *If the priority of your marriage is not where you want it to be, what is one action you can take to move toward prioritizing your marriage?*

WEEK 49

HOLY SEX

For this reason, a man will leave his father and his mother, and will be joined to his wife. And they will become one flesh.

Genesis 2:24 NIV

When God created the universe and all that is in it, one of his most beautiful gifts was that of sex. But sex is also a gift that Satan has done his best to degrade, counterfeit, and manipulate into something that is grotesque, rooted in selfishness, and a false promise of "love."

I'm sure that some in the church have unwittingly aided Satan's cause. Sex has been made to be something dirty that "good" people don't talk about. We simply tell the unmarried, "Don't! It's a sin." When they get married, we say, "Okay, you can do it now." We have stifled communication about this incredible gift that God designed for marriage to the point that even married couples are unsure how to talk about it. Let's change that!

I love this quote by Sheila Wray Gregoire in her book *The Great Sex Rescue: The Lies You've Been Taught and How to Recover What God Intended*:

> Great sex is the fulfillment of a longing for intimacy, for connection, to be completely and utterly bare in every way before each other. Yes, baring ourselves physically for sex is necessary, but that is not the only kind of baring that real sex involves. It's also a baring of our souls, a deep hunger for connection, a longing to be completely consumed by the other—while also bringing intense pleasure to both of you.[10]

I don't know about you, but that's the kind of sex I want to have. I think that's what God designed sex to be like and we see that in Song of Solomon. We talked earlier about physical intimacy, and married sex is the ultimate in physical intimacy. It is rooted in a love that is open, caring, and unselfish, and has a desire to bring pleasure and satisfaction to your spouse. That is something that the act of intercourse outside of the marriage covenant can never be.

Here is another crazy thought: Married sex can be an act of worship. Bible scholar D. A. Carson writes, "It is as if the only pleasure and intimacy in this life that comes close to anticipating the pleasure of the church and her Lord being perfectly united on the last day is the sexual union of a good marriage."[11] And in *Sex and the Supremacy of Christ*, John Piper writes, "God created us with sexual passion so that there would be language to describe what it means to cleave to him in love and what it means to turn away from him to others"[12] and "God made us powerfully sexual so that he would be more deeply knowable. We were given the

---

10 Sheila Wray Gregoire, *The Great Sex Rescue: The Lies You've Been Taught and How to Recover What God Intended* (Grand Rapids, MI: Baker Books, 2021), 13.

11 D. A. Carson, *Love in Hard Places* (Wheaton, IL: Crossway, 2002), 191.

12 John Piper, *Sex and the Supremacy of Christ* (Wheaton, IL: Crossway, 2005), 28.

power to know each other sexually so that we might have some hint of what it will be like to know Christ supremely."[13] Wow! When was the last time you heard that in church?

So, let's start a dialogue about married sex. It may not be the most important part of a godly marriage, but it is a big one. Let's first consider some of the myths about sex that our culture has perpetuated.

- *Married sex is bad or boring.* Wrong. According to researchgate.com, monogamous married couples express the highest levels of sexual satisfaction.[14]

- *Good sex comes naturally.* No, it doesn't. Great sex, like a great marriage, requires intentionality. As in all aspects of marriage, we can learn to be better, even in sex.

- *In a good marriage, sex will be problem-free.* We wish this was true. Know that issues with your sex life will probably arise. Be sure to talk about them and find a solution together.

- *Sex is primarily for the man.* God created sex for both men and women to enjoy and find fulfillment.

Now Adam knew Eve his wife, and she conceived. (Genesis 4:1 ESV)

I have entered my garden, my treasure, my bride! I gather myrrh with my spices and eat honeycomb with my honey. I drink wine with my milk. Oh, lover and beloved, eat and drink! Yes, drink deeply of your love! (Song of Solomon 5:1 NLT)

---

13   Ibid., 30.
14   https://www.researchgate.net/publication/332418012_Sexual_Satisfaction_in_Monogamous_Nonmonogamous_and_Unpartnered_Sexual_Minority_Women_in_the_US

COUPLES ♥ CHALLENGE

♥ *On a scale of 1–10, with 1 = nonexistent and 10 = heaven on earth, how would you rate your sexual intimacy?*

♥ *Are there any myths or misconceptions about sex that you have believed? Discuss together.*

♥ *Does your spouse know what you like and what you don't when it comes to sexual intimacy? (Remember question #5 of the 5 Questions from Week 16.)*

♥ *Do you feel comfortable talking with your spouse about sex? Why or why not?*

THE "WHY" OF SEX

How beautiful you are, my love, and how pleasing in all your delightful and satisfying ways. Your stature is as elegant as a date palm tree, and your breasts are sweet, attractive, and round like clusters of its fruit. I say, "I will climb the palm tree; I will take hold of its fruit." May your breasts be like clusters of grapes, the fragrance of your mouth like fresh apples.

Song of Solomon 7:6–8 VOICE

When it comes to sex, the culture we live in says that God, the Bible, and Christianity are old-fashioned and out of touch. They believe God and the Bible are anti-sex. They could not be further from the truth. Does the Song of Solomon really sound like God is against sex? God is not anti-sex; he is against the misuse of sex. He created sex, and he knows how it is best experienced.

So, why did God create sex? We know it's the primary method of procreation, but God could have had us laying eggs. (Thank goodness he didn't.) Instead, he created the most intimate act we can ever experience with someone. Let's consider some of the reasons God created sex for marriage.

- Sex is an act of worship. When done the right way—unveiled, giving and not taking, focusing on the needs and desires of our spouse over and above our own—sex is the culmination of who we are as a couple physically, emotionally, and spiritually. It glorifies God when that is our experience.

- Sex is an act of creation that brings forth life. It helps fulfill God's plan to raise godly generations.

- Sex is the physical representation of the oneness we have spiritually and emotionally.

- Sex is designed to bond a husband and wife together. Science tells us that when we have sex, our bodies release hormones that create a connection and bond between the husband and wife.

- Sex is for pleasure. We are to delight in each other's bodies. The Song of Solomon is an affirmation of this truth.

- Sex is meant to image the intimate relationship between Christ and his bride, the church.

Now, based on the purposes for this incredible gift of sex, what are some truths about sex that flow from its purposes?

- Trust is essential for great sex. When we can trust our spouse, we feel safe and secure and can abandon ourselves to passion.

- Sex values the other person for who they are, not just for what they can give us.

- Sex ought to be a priority. Both partners should desire sex, even if at different levels, and it is an important part of a healthy marriage.

- Sex should be pure. It is designed only for marriage relationships.

- Sex should be freely given, never pressured. There's no place for manipulation, threats, or coercion.

- We should not settle for an unfulfilling sex life in our marriage. If there are issues, we need to find the solution.

Sex, as God designed it to be, is beautiful. Great sex derives from a passion for each other rooted in deep trust and Christlike love for each other.

> God saw all that he had made, and it was very good. (Genesis 1:31 NIV)

COUPLES ♥ CHALLENGE

♥ *What do you think about the idea that sex is an act of worship? Do you feel uncomfortable thinking about God and sex?*

♥ *Have you ever thought about why God created sex? Do the reasons for sex mentioned above help you see it in a different way than you have before? Why or why not?*

♥ *Are you satisfied with the sexual intimacy that you and your spouse have? What are some things you wish you had more or less of?*

WHEN SEX ISN'T GOOD

> *Dnd we know that for those who love God all things work together for good, for those who are called according to his purpose .... He who did not spare his own Son but gave him up for us all, how will he not also with him graciously give us all things?*
>
> **Romans 8:28, 32 ESV**

Why do we settle for less than the best that God desires for us? When it comes to sex, I think it is because we don't see sex for what God created it to be. Whether it's because we have been warped by hearing about sex in such a negative way or we have bought the lie that sex is not supposed to be good, so many couples settle for less than an awesome sex life.

We don't have to. Sex can be a glorious expression of the love we share. Do not settle for less than God's best!

Our sexual intimacy, like every other area of our marriage, can run into problems and conflicts. We usually don't have a problem talking about our finances or communication issues. But when it comes to sex, many couples don't know how to talk about it. If you are having issues with sexual intimacy in your marriage, know that you're not alone. Let's look at some issues that couples can face.

Emotional Issues

- If you feel disconnected in other areas of your marriage

- If you are overly stressed

- If you don't feel safe

- If you feel like you are being used

- If you are depressed

Situational Issues

- If you are too tired for sex

- If there's a lack of time

- If there is no privacy

- If your work schedules conflict

- If you are overloaded and your mind won't let you relax

Physical Issues

- If there is physical illness

- If sex is painful or uncomfortable

- If hormonal or age-related changes are present

- If there's a normal ebb and flow of sexual desires

- If there's an inability to reach climax

These are some of the many issues faced, and there are certainly others. If you're dealing with any of these, seek a solution. The first thing to do is to talk about it with your spouse. Work out a solution together. If the root is emotional, see a counselor. If the root is situational, figure out a way to schedule some time for sexual intimacy. If there's a physical issue such as pain or sexual disfunction, talk to your doctor. The main thing is to not ignore it. Sex is too important to not address the issues that are creating a problem.

Jesus said that he came so we could live a full and abundant life. That includes your sexual relationship in marriage. Is sex the most important thing in your marriage? No, but it is an important part, so if it's not what you want, figure out how to change that.

> Casting all your anxieties on him because he cares for you. (1 Peter 5:7 ESV)

> Now to the God who can do so many awe-inspiring things, immeasurable things, things greater than we ever could ask or imagine through the power at work in us." (Ephesians 3:20 VOICE)

COUPLES ♥ CHALLENGE

♥ If you're not in the habit of talking about sex, doing so can be hard. Try starting with something like this short quiz. Each of you answer the questions. Then talk about your answers. Where is there agreement? Where do you differ?

> How often would you like to have sex?
>
> Are you having sex as often as you would like, more than you would like, or less than you would like?
>
> When and where do you most enjoy having sex?
>
> Are there things that make you more interested in having sex?
>
> What is one thing you might want to try or do differently in your sex life?

♥ Are you experiencing any of the emotional, situational, or physical issues listed above? Make a list and start working together to solve the issue(s).

♥ Set goals for your sex life just as you would for other areas of your marriage.

REKINDLE THE FIRE

The fire on the altar shall be kept burning,
it shall not be allowed to go out.

Leviticus 6:12 NLT

I hope and pray, as you read this closing devotional in our 52-week couples challenge, that you know the fire is burning brightly in your marriage. But what if it's not? What can you do to rekindle the fire?

- Determine not to let it stay that way.
- Remove the old ashes.

To take the first step, start doing what needs to be done. Don't wait. It doesn't matter who makes the first move; what matters is that you start to move. Leviticus 6:10 talks about how the priest had to clean out the old ashes. If he didn't, the fire would not be able to continue to burn; the buildup would extinguish the flame.

Our marriage is like that too. We must clean out the ashes. We must deal with issues and not allow them to build up and snuff out the flame. If they have built up, then we must do the work of getting rid of the ashes. Whatever that may entail, we must remove the ashes. So ...

- Remind yourself of God's purpose for marriage.

- Don't expect your marriage to be something God did not design it to be.

God's purpose for marriage is for it to reflect the relationship between Christ and his bride, the church. It is meant to provide incredible intimacy, the wonder of sharing lives that complement one another, and a partnering together in our journey through this life. But God does not intend for our spouse to meet the deepest needs of our hearts or to be our everything. Only God can fill those needs. To summarize. . .

- Remember what you loved at first.

- Do the things you did at first.

Sometimes when things are hard, we get so focused on what is not right that we forget what we loved at the beginning. We did certain things when we first started dating, or early in our relationship, that were a part of why we ended up together. Do those again.

- Be intentional about focusing on your spouse in a positive way.

- Demonstrate or verbalize one thing that is loving, affirming, appreciative, or kind toward your spouse every day.

We must choose the way we think about our spouse and our marriage. If all our thoughts dwell on the negative, the issues, and what we don't have, then our mindset and emotions will remain negative. Intentionally choosing to focus on what we do appreciate and what we are thankful for will allow our emotions to soften and we will begin to see more of what we do have, not less.

- Out-serve your spouse.

- Determine yours to be a marriage on mission.

Think about the last thing Jesus did with his disciples prior to his crucifixion. He wrapped a towel around his waist, got down on his knees, and washed their feet (John 13:1–15). The very feet of those he created. Jesus took on the role of the lowest servant, showing how we are to love one another. There is no harder place to love consistently than in our marriage. We see, feel, and smell dirty feet. How might God be asking us to serve our spouse out of love for them?

A marriage on mission is a marriage that knows that it is more than simply a marriage. We resolutely see beyond the temporal to how God desires to use our unique marriage to impact the kingdom of God. This will look different for every believing couple. A marriage on mission for God's kingdom will embrace the gift of having a partner to lean on, challenge us, and keep us moving forward in our walk through this life.

Kingdom marriages will leave footprints for eternity. We want that for our marriage, and we know you want that for yours. It is work, but with God all things are possible.

> In the morning, after the priest on duty has put on his official linen clothing and linen undergarments, he must clean out the ashes of the burnt offering and put them beside the altar. (Leviticus 6:10 NLT)

> Whoever drinks of the water that I give him will never be thirsty again. The water that I give will become in him a spring of water welling up to eternal life. (John 4:13–14 ESV)

COUPLES ♥ CHALLENGE

♥ *Talk about the "fire" in your marriage. Is it burning brightly? Do you have ashes that might need to be removed?*

♥ *Do you have unmet expectations or frustrations? Have you shared them?*

♥ *Think about one positive thing you used to do when you were first together. Are you still doing it? If not, why? Start doing it again.*

♥ *Tell each other one thing that attracted you to the other.*

♥ *For thirty days, do or say one thing that shows your spouse what you appreciate, are thankful for, love, or respect about them.*

♥ *Talk about what a marriage on mission means for you.*

Made in the USA
Columbia, SC
02 July 2024

37915564R00124